Josip   Gabre

HOW I BEAT CANCER

(AND HOW YOU CAN PREVENT IT)

D1227935

Josip Gabre

Josip Gabre was born the 20th of February 1927 in Tisno Croatia. He writes poetry and prose. He has been published in Croatian magazines, weeklies and dailies in the old country and in ethnic publications in Canada and the USA. Also he has participated in several group anthologies.

He won first prize with his short story THE BREAD in Sarajevo in 1988, and also with his poem BEFORE THE STORM in 1989. Josip's largest published collection of poems and short stories to date are in his non fiction novel "THE SEED FROM THE STONE" which is now being translated into English.

Presently he is working on a nonfiction trilogy.

This book I dedicate to my granddaughter

D A P H N E

Josip Gabre

Author

Josip Gabre
4605 Donegal Dr. Unit # 11
Mississauga, Ont.
L5M 4X7   Canada

Tel. (905) 828 5845

Josip Gabre

DISCLAIMER

This book is not intended to replace the service of a physician. It is a descriptive experience of a man who cured himself from cancer. In a way it is a critical examination of orthodox, alternate and potential cancer therapies, as well as a look at the politics of cancer. Any use of the information set forth in the following pages is at the reader's discretion. No statement included in this book should be considered as medical advice. The author assumes no responsibility for any decisions made by the reader regarding cancer treatment.

TABLE OF CONTENTS

FOREWORD

To write about cancer and how someone cured himself of it, is as diversified as the physiological, psychological and all other differences among humans. Perhaps this is the reason we still do not have a universal cure for cancer. Maybe we are still wandering in the dark, and do not want to realize how and why it strikes. Unfortunately, I had a chance to observe cancer first hand, long before it struck me. I believe it was my destiny. Trying to help others, I prepared myself to struggle against it. Everything I learned about cancer at the time was so discouraging, that, in the very beginning, as probably others have experienced, I had doubts about my healing.

How do we get cancer? Unfortunately, medical studies offer no answers to this question. There are so many explanations and all of them are so confusing. I had read many books about cancer, and common sense led me to accept the following explanations given by Drs. Ewan Cameron and Linus Pauling.

During the creation of new cells, which in healthy humans, the immune system is in control of, disorders happen. When, for some reason our immune system fails, malignant cells multiply without control and jeopardize the rest of the system. This seemed very logical to me. Other explanations seemed to side track and

Josip Gabre

lead to confusion as to the causes and the cures of cancer.

Having read many books about cancer, I found statements by many prominent doctors who spoke openly about its causes. More or less they agreed with the explanations given by Doctors Cameron and Pauling, and the recommendations on how to cure it. However, these recommendations on how to cure cancer are in dispute with those recommended by the medical authorities. I also discovered that all these courageous individuals had unfortunate endings to their careers. They were condemned and persecuted by their colleagues and institutions to which they had until then, belonged. In this way, a great injustice is done to conscientious doctors and to their patients alike, for it makes a healthy relationship between them an impossiblility.

Speaking from experience, I learned that a healthy and open doctor-patient relationship is a very valid factor in combatting any illness, especially cancer. Many patients have problems discussing with their physician an alternate cure for cancer, which is unacceptable by the Canadian Cancer Society or Canadian Medical Association. This is the first stumbling block for all those stricken by disease. They are forced to accept treatments recommended by their physicians. On the other hand, those physicians who would like to test alternate ways are forbidden to cure their patients in a way that their personal experience and consciences would choose.

I have to ask a logical question: Is this Institutional response in the best interest of the patient, or does it limit the physician doing his or her utmost for the patient? Obviously, whatever the answer, it is sure to be contraversial.

We know that medical authorities recommend three kinds of therapies and these are: surgery, chemotherapy and radiation. Unfortunately none of these are giving satisfactory results, and we continualy ask, is it worth putting a patient through such torture? Psychologically, it then follows that the patient falls into apathy, when he/she is sure that from that mindset there is only one exit ... death!

There is no evidence documented in print, but often such therapies are shortening the patient's life rather than prolonging it. Why the medical authorities still recommend only these three kinds of treatments is a mystery. Thus exists the dilemma of still having more questions than answers. Proponents of other directions of research, are harassed, and persecuted as well. The reasons for this remain unanswered and obscure.

Frequently, we hear that cancer is the product of viruses. I found in one magazine that cancer can be transmitted sexually. I don't want to argue this statement, but to me, it sounds strange. Today, it appears that, everything unexplainable is proclaimed cancer. Research done by Doctors Virginia Livingston and Eleanor Jackson is pointing out that there are certain tuberculosis-like microbes present in every source of cancer. The same discovery had been made in many laboratories and was always considered an infection. Doctor Donsbach, in his book SUPER HEALTH, mentions that those microbes are found in the blood of cancer patients, but cannot be transmitted. In the same book he says that such micro organisms can't develop in a system with the normal metabolism. In the early 1930's, Dr. Royal Rife isolated cancer microbes and 100% successfully cured terminal cancer patients. His work was sabotaged and suppressed to this day, and so was the work of others. What does this research tell us? Is cancer a virus or not? Due to incorrect attitudes from cancer authorities we still have no conclusive answers.

Are there any discoveries in that direction? Are these microbes appearing as predecessors to cancer or are they post cancer effects? If research were to organize in a different direction, then no doubt, we would have better answers to this enigma.

Going back to the theory of Drs. Cameron and Pauling, and many others as well, the human system, which by itself, when healthy, is perfection in mutual coordination, with the motto: "one for all, and all for one," functions impeccably, immune to all sickness and of cancer as well. Each cell, gland and organ has to fulfil a certain function to make the human body work properly. That is to say, in our highly organized and perfect body, where each cell is subjected to a common interest, something went wrong.

I am not a medical doctor, nor a scientist able to discuss technically the functions of cells. Common sense is leading me to ask the questions: If there are differences among cells in the same way as there are among humans, is it possible to find a universal cure for cancer that would satisfy the conditions of all individuals? Does this mean, that we cannot and must not hope, that someday a cure for cancer will be found? We have seen, from the research of doctors Pauling and Cameron, where the key answer for our research is. The immune system, which is responsible for the development of cells, has to be brought into its optimal functional state. Many researchers, directly or indirectly, gave us this answer. Why then, are we still wandering in the dark and side tracking? Why is cancer still treated with methods which are destroying the human immune system? Where is the logic?

Cancer can be cured, and I am living proof of it. Why can't research be more inclusionary to include alternative thought processes, to help us get out of this no win situation? There are many examples of how individuals have cured themselves in an 'unconventional way', and I am one of them. Looking for a cure, I met many others who cured themselves, although medical doctors had written them off.

Has medical science made any attempt to investigate these 'other' possibilities? If not, this means that the problem isn't approached in a way to satisfy the diversity of every human being. Is medical science self-denying the full insight to the causes of cancer? This may be the best explanation for why we still haven't got a universal cure for cancer. Is medical science so advanced, that nothing can be explained? Will a cure ever be found for cancer? Looking at the situation as it is now, it is very difficult to find logical answers. In my case, I have seen much hypocrisy from medical doctors. In this book I will touch on situations where I was not told everything that I should have known, so that I might have accepted or refused some treatments recommended me. If there had been any sincerity and frankness from my doctors, I would be in a much better situation today.

After so much agonizing and after such a bitter experience, I had no other choice but to believe in the theory of our bodily structure, cell activity, and the immune system, as explained by Drs. Cameron and Pauling. Our immune system acts as a vigilant policeman for the benefit of our body, and immediately destroys any cells that break the motto: "all for one, and one for all." When that police force in our system fails, cancer cells spread around to harm their environment, and in turn, harm human life. The approach to cancer healing *by strengthening our immune system,* which, by the abuse of our body, weakened by food, air or water pollution, stress, radiation exposure, or any other irregularities to which we are exposed these days, is most logical. Describing my illness and how I conquered it, is total proof of the validity of this theory. I believe that it was this one fact that helped me the most in my healing, even when my doctors had given up on me.

I sincerely wish you the patience, open-mindedness and faith required to survive any of your present afflictions or those which may arise in your future.

Josip Gabre

CHAPTER ONE

(COSTLY DECISIONS)

After lunch, on Thursday July the seventh 1983, I went to the bathroom, and noticed that my urine was a little darker than usual. I thought that perhaps I had eaten something that caused this to occur. Nevertheless, I didn't like what I saw. The colour of the urine wasn't like when we eat something different and our kidneys extract an excess of vitamins, minerals or other substances. I could hardly wait until the next time I had to go to the bathroom. To my great relief, this time my urine was normal.

The next day, July the 8th, my wife and I went to, as we do every Friday, the Kensington market to purchase fish. Upon my arrival home I went to the bathroom, and to my dismay and horror, my urine was completely black. Greatly distressed, I called my family doctor at home. He suggested that I go immediately to a Downtown Hospital. I went by subway and it took a long time. Upon my arrival I had to wait some time until the resident doctor from the urology department arrived. The situation with my urine was much better now, but the doctor said that I still had blood in it. He made an appointment with the urologist for a cystoscopic examination for Tuesday July the 12th.

Josip Gabre

At first, the cystoscopic examination showed nothing. Nevertheless, perhaps guided by experience, Dr. urologist was not satisfied until he had used the largest lens he had. With that lens he found something hidden in the upper front of the bladder above the draining canal. According to his findings it was as small as a needle point. He recommended treatment with Bacillus Calmette - Guerin (BCG) vaccine. As the Dr. urologist explained to his young colleagues who were under his supervision, the BCG vaccine was used with this type of problem. "Do not ask me how," he said, "but it is believed that this vaccine is healing this kind of problem".

The BCG is a vaccine, which was used to suppress tuberculosis before the discovery of penicillin. It stimulates the body's defense system to oppose tuberculosis and cancer as well. This is what medical science has to say about it, but it is a subordinate treatment, not a real therapy against cancer. All this I found out much later when I collected the material for this book. From Dr. urologist's explanation to his young colleagues, apparently he wasn't sure what he was doing. I was a Guinea Pig, and lack of awareness about cancer was evident, by all the parties concerned.

Looking back on my problem, how the cancer developed, and which methods were used for its cure, many things are becoming clearer to me. Now, I still don't understand why my doctor used these methods. If BCG is used to suppress tuberculosis, due to enhancement of the immune system by inoculation, how it can work in the bladder, just by squirting it in, is still unclear to me. My lack of knowledge hindered me from scrutinizing the methods recommended and then used. Naturally I don't blame my Dr. urologist for it, for he did everything he could, but, as it can be seen, either everything from the beginning was wrong, or it simply didn't work for me?

Are there any other differences between cancer cells and healthy ones in distress, caused by infections and inflammation, other than the speed of their multiplications, characteristic for such a sickness?

If only the speed of reproduction is considered, then there can be much confusion. When our system is in danger, healthy cells reproduce, perhaps even faster than cancer cells, to be able to fight the disease. From what I have read, heard and experienced about cancer, I firmly believe this theory is correct. It is obvious everything has not yet been said about cancer, and can be wrongly diagnosed?

At the onset of my illness, I had no answer to any of these questions, and I allowed my doctor to do whatever he thought was necessary, without asking questions. Mr. Barry Lynes, in one of his lectures about cancer treatment with ultra frequency rays beyond the spectrum of the known oscillations, said: "We trust our plumber that he will do a good job, but in our doctor we believe". As with everybody else, I was motivated by an unquestionable confidence in my doctor. I had faith in him and put my life in his hands. If I had known what I know now about cancer, I would have asked many more questions, and most certainly would never have accepted the treatments.

The BCG vaccine was injected into my bladder through the penis. I had to retain urine for two hours to help the BCG vaccine dissolve whatever was in my bladder in order to cure my problem. It was satisfactory for the first few treatments. After that I got an inflammation of the tube and the entire bladder, and it was unbearable to retain my urine for two hours.

Josip Gabre

I complained about it, and my Dr. urologist postponed the treatment for several weeks. During that time the pain disappeared, but it reappeared when the therapy resumed.

After the sixth therapy was done, a cystoscopic examination was performed again, and it was then found that disease encompassed my entire bladder. In other words, my bladder was destroyed. A biopsy sample was taken and sent to the laboratory for analysis and it was found that my entire bladder contained a huge cancerous tumour. It was then obvious that the BCG not only didn't cure my cancer, it apparently helped it to spread much faster than ever.

I received a telephone call from Dr. urologist's office. His secretary told me that the doctor wanted to see me within one week, when he returned from vacation. I knew exactly what was happening, and I said to my wife:
"You'll see, I have cancer."
"Don't be silly," she said.
"If nothing else," I said, "they would tell me what it is. But if he has called me to talk, it can be nothing less than to tell me that I have cancer".

She didn't argue with me and was very concerned, as I was. We waited for that appointment, and did not discuss it any further; but the matter did not leave our minds.

Two months from my urine discovery on September the 7th, I had the appointment with my Dr. urologist. In the examining room, before he appeared, separately, several young doctors visited me. Repeatedly I had to relate my entire health history. I felt as though I was being interrogated for a crime I had never committed. Finally, Dr. urologist arrived.

For the first time, I noticed that he had difficulty talking to me. He said that he would cure me, because my case was easily curable, never mentioning what kind of therapy he would use. He knew that if he mentioned it, I would understand what kind of disease I had. I believe that it is the most difficult task that a doctor has to face, knowing that there is little he can do for his patient. I understood everything, and I asked: "Doctor, do I have cancer?"

He hesitated for a moment trying to find the right words, not once looking at me.

"Doctor," I pleaded, "tell me the truth. You know, it won't help me if you deny it."

"Yes," he said, "you have cancer."

The diagnosis was: *"Papillary transitional cell carcinoma grade III/IV, with the invasion of submucosa and smooth muscle."*

He tried to convince me that for this type of cancer, a cure existed. I listened blindly not understanding anything; my head filled with noises to the point I thought it would explode. I remember being barely able to hear him.

It's hard to say what I felt then. Within myself I felt a big emptiness. "So, this is it," I thought, and at that very moment, I felt strangely relaxed. Fear? No, I felt no fear. This wasn't the first time that I faced death. Instead, I had felt some kind of satisfaction. Satisfaction that everything would end, and very quickly too. With that, all my sufferings, physical and emotional, would disappear. It sounds so unreal today, when I think back about it. Perhaps the shock was so great, it numbed all my senses and I felt nothing. In such a state of mind, not being fully aware of what was going on, I was very calm.

5   *Josip Gabre*

In a state of daze I followed the discussion but I felt as though it was about somebody else. I heard everything and nothing simultaneously. I understood everything and yet did not understand anything at all, because mentally I wasn't there; therefore, the conversation was not about me, but about somebody else, unknown to me, justifying my calmness.

My urologist then explained to me what he would do to cure me, and I listened to him with one ear only. I knew, there was no cure for me. Everything that would be done would torture me more and more. I had to give him an answer, but what kind of answer could I give him? If only I could believe in what he was saying. I remembered the pain that I had suffered during the BCG therapy, and still suffered, after the therapy had ended. The Dr. urologist explained thoroughly how radiation treatment would have no effect here and that the only solutions were the surgery or chemotherapy. With the surgery I would live the rest of my life with an ileal loop and a plastic pouch. For how long? With the chemotherapy, I would live in pain while my hair would fall out, with intestines damaged, and not able to digest food. Toxins would attack all of my vital organs, and I knew that my body would be unable to combat the disease. Can anybody combat this disease?

Thousands of questions swarmed in my head, but on any of them I had no answer. My mind screamed "accept the cure, that the doctor is offering you," but something else within myself rebelled. I heard a strange voice deep down inside. It felt so strong. It rejected all of the doctors' reasonings, and all his suggestions, even though I knew that he meant them with best intentions.

Quickly, my life passed before me. What a paradox! When he is young, man never thinks about death. He volunteers to go to war. When in an open field, under deadly machine-gun fire, he runs toward a stone, a tree, anything that would protect him. I needed such a rock, such a fraudulent shelter and I didn't have it. I needed that solitary rock, bush, or wall to dash to with all my might, even if I would drop dead halfway there. That false hope wasn't there, and I faced death. I had nothing then with which to fight back and save my life, as I had so often before.

From my point of view medical science was sending me to the gallows. I was condemned to death, and all that the Dr. urologist offered me, was a choice which way to die. The death, which was so close many times before, and didn't get to me, was once again coming very slowly but surely and I saw it very clearly. I saw it through all the things that I had earned with hard and honest work, and now had to leave behind. I also saw it through my family that I loved more than myself, through my friends, and through my relatives. I saw it through my unfinished plans, which I had hoped to accomplish sometime in the future. Before this, I had never appreciated my life. Now, it was so precious to me. It was precious, even with all its faults and suffering. I loved it because of my family, my wife Mladenka and my daughter Jerina. I loved it because of my hobbies, night schools, through which I completed grade twelve, electronics, and a host of many other things. I loved it because of my poems and many, many more things good and bad. Everything had to end, and I knew that. Yet I felt that it wasn't quite the time. Death was coming slowly and painfully. This time I couldn't run away, nor could I fight back.

Dr. urologist waited. He is a very busy physician. He never wastes any time. With a pocket cassette-recorder, he directs the activities of his two secretaries. He goes from one examining room to another, from one patient to another, like a hurricane; sometime it's difficult to talk to him. Young doctors follow him around, and from him they learn. From him they learn how to save time. But at this crucial moment in time, he was patient. He leaned against the desk, and was waiting for my answer. Should I trust him? Should I put my life in his hands?

7   *Josip Gabre*

I was so confused. I felt as though there were two people inside me. One was saying "YES," and another one, deep down inside, stronger than the first, was screaming "NO." My doctor gave me no guarantees. He couldn't guarantee anything, because medical science gave him nothing to use against the cancer. It wasn't his fault. He offered what he had, but that wasn't enough. Had he said: "Joe, go home and wait until you die, I can't help you or I can make you suffer even more, and at the end, the results would be just the same." If only he could have said so, he would have done so much more for me. But he couldn't do that. Patiently he waited and I used his time, his precious time needed for his other patients. I sighed:

"Doctor, forgive me, I don't want to take any of the therapies, you have offered me," I said.

Was that my voice? Did I hear it properly? Where did I get such a strength? Was I refusing that sheltering rock that would protect me from death. Yes, but this rock wasn't solid. It wasn't made from strong material to stop the blow. It was built from a weak, transparent material, which could penetrate a child's sling. There was no hope for me. I don't know why, but it reminded me of a situation from World War II.

It happened often: I had to jump from behind a protected position to another one. Suddenly I felt some unseen hand grab and hold me. I swear, I felt it physically. A few seconds later, the ground that I had to run across, was sprayed with machine gun bullets.

This time I had the same feeling. Something was telling me not to accept the doctor's offer, for there was no hope. I followed that instinct without question.

"My friend, you are wrong," he said.

"I know, doctor," I said calmly, "I am doing it on purpose."

"One day you will bleed, and that will be the end. I am trying to save your life."

"I know, doctor, but that is exactly what I don't want."

"What?"

"Doctor," I said, "at this very moment I hate my life. I will try to find a cure by myself."

Did he believe in his promises? Would he save my life? If only I could believe that! If he were so sure, why wasn't he more persistent in trying to convince me to accept his cure?

What could I do? Maybe he was right. Maybe I had to accept one of these therapies. Then, the removal of the bladder with surgery was the best solution, because the cancer hadn't spread yet outside it. From what I had learned from books, chemotherapy was not acceptable at all. According to medical science, chemotherapy is a cytotoxic poison that kills cancer cells that are multiplying rapidly. But is this true? Nobody could guarantee that the poison that would kill the cancer cells, would not kill good cells as well and much faster too. I, who had tuberculosis and diabetes and had undergone surgery nine times, knew what it meant when the system weakens and has no power to fight disease. No, chemotherapy was out of the question. I knew, if I accepted it, that would be the end of all my efforts to beat cancer. Radiation therapy would probably have been effective if applied at first, before the cancer had covered the whole bladder.

As I stated before, BCG is a kind of anti-tuberculosis vaccine. With it, Dr. Hans Nieper tried to stimulate the immune system. I found in the same text that, along with BCG, Dr. Nieper used a mild chemotherapy treatment, and a special diet, to replace lost elements (phosphorus, zinc, iron, potassium and copper). In their book "Cancer and vitamin C", Drs. Pauling and Cameron talk about treatments with BCG, and underline the fact that such treatments have side effects. I didn't like what they had to say about BCG. Nowhere did I find statistics of how many patients' Dr. Nieper cured with his method.

Today, if advised to take that therapy again, after reading about it and after such a bitter experience, categorically, I would refuse it. Why? I am absolutely convinced that the BCG therapy destroyed my bladder. Furthermore, I strongly believe that if I had refused that therapy, I would be in a much better situation today, and in far less pain. Unfortunately, I didn't know all these facts at the time and I accepted what my doctor suggested. I accepted the BCG therapy without much thought, and I realized that I had made a gross mistake.

CHAPTER TWO

(FRIENDS, OMENS AND COUNTRYMEN)

Quite some time before I got cancer, at St. Mary's Drug Store at Yonge and Grosvenor Streets, I bought a book written by Maria Treben, titled "GOD'S MEDICINE." In that book I found information that many people cured themselves of cancer with herbs: Yarrow, Calendula and Nettle, with the poultice of Swedish bitter. I decided to use these herbs and see what would happen. I am sure that it was instinct, more than common sense, which led me to take these herbs. My doctor gave me no guaranty to cure my illness. In a way, Maria Treben, with her method, did guarantee healing the kind of cancer that I suffered from. Maybe that helped me to decide more than anything else. She offered something that medical science never did. How realistic was it? Everyone will have their own opinion, especially medical doctors, but I had no other choice.

My urologist insisted that I come to see him in October. Through his secretary, he stressed the importance of that visit. Realizing how stubborn I was, and how decided to self-destruct, I am sure he doubted that I would keep the appointment. Perhaps he was motivated by something else, I don't know. I am not a medical doctor and therefore I am not able to comprehend the mysteries of that profession. I promised him I would be back as he requested, and assured him that my word is the best guaranty he could have. If I decided differently, I would keep my word just the same, no matter what.

I went straight back to work. Slowly I walked those few blocks. I needed time to think. I knew that my friends would ask what the doctor had told me. Everybody expected the worst. Regardless, nobody talked about it, but one could sense it in the air and everybody was concerned. They had observed the development with my BCG therapy, and that was enough to comprehend the situation. Besides, I told them everything that was happening.

When I told them what the result of the analysis was, silence prevailed. Everybody had a long face, and I was talking about the problem without difficulty, as though I was talking about any daily happening. Still, I couldn't comprehend the truth. I couldn't believe it was happening to me, and tried to forget all about it. Regardless, I couldn't avoid their concerned looks. Dr. Bob Chapman, who lost his mother to cancer, stood aside, listening to my conversation with others. Everybody was trying to console me, but he never said one word. When everybody left, he approached me and offered me a chair. He felt depressed talking about it, but he wanted to help me, knowing how much I was suffering.

"Relax," he said.

He looked straight ahead and waited for some time, not knowing what else to say. I was silent too. Still looking downwards he started talking as though he wasn't addressing me.

"You know, I lost my mother the same way."

"I know. I heard about it. I am sorry Bob, really. I lost my mother too, when I was only two and a half years old. A Mother is never too old, and we miss her all the time, and although it happened so long ago, I know your feelings."

"Thank you," he said. "She suffered for fifteen years from cancer and tuberculosis simultaneously. It is hard to say which killed her, the cancer or tuberculosis. I know that once she started with chemotherapy treatment, she didn't last long. Her condition deteriorated rapidly, accompanied by some effects that chemotherapy carries with it."

"And she didn't last long?"

"That is right, she didn't last long."

"My doctor suggested the same therapy for me. What do you think? Should I accept it or not?"

"I don't know. I am not qualified."

"Your mother lived with tuberculosis and cancer for fifteen years. When she started the chemotherapy treatment, she didn't last one year. Is that so?"

"Yes, it was that way."

"Do you think she would have lived longer without chemotherapy?"

"Maybe not, because several organs were affected, but I don't really know. I am not qualified. It is hard to say."

"What would you, as a friend, suggest that I do? Should I accept chemotherapy?"

"Joe, don't ask me that. You know, I am not qualified to give such advice. And again... my experience, you know how it is."

"Yes, I do. My head is as huge as a barrel. I am trying not to think about it, but I can't help it. Wherever I go, whatever I do, I am reminded of it. I feel as though I am in a coffin, and the boys are coming to pay me their last respects. I know, I shouldn't think that way, but, believe me or not, there is no hope for me."

"You are exaggerating."

"Am I? Your mother lived fifteen years without any therapies. Then, when she submitted to chemotherapy, she died. Is it so?"

"Yes, that is correct, but you are still a young man, and physically very strong too."

"My doctor told me, one day I will hemorrhage and that will be the end. If I take chemotherapy, the result will be just the same. I don't know what is worse. If only I had somebody to ask for advice? I can't go to my family doctor. If I ask him for an opinion he will take the doctor's side, and recommend that I take chemotherapy. That is exactly what I don't want to do. I am so confused that I don't know what is right and what is wrong. You see, I am asking you for an opinion, because of your experience, but you don't feel qualified to give me one. There is no advice that is good for me. I have to choose death. One way or another, the result is the same - Death! If I asked you, Bob, what would you do in my position, the answer would be the same: "I don't know!" You see, that is the worse part of it. Wherever I go to ask for advice, I can't get any. The boys feel sorry for me. You heard them saying that I shouldn't worry about the job. They would do it for me. Can't you understand, that is what hurts the most? Apparently I am already dead, and yet, I am still alive. How? Don't ask me, because I don't know anymore."

"What answer did you give to your doctor?"

"I refused all therapies that he offered me."

"Oh boy, that is a harsh decision. Can't you think it over? Sleep on it and make a decision tomorrow."

"Yes, it is a harsh decision, but the only one I can think of."

This conversation made me so uneasy. It is difficult when somebody pities you, especially a friend. As much as I tried to smother my feelings, as much as I tried to think about something else and forget what was coming, his comment laid on my heart like a rock. As long as I could breathe and fight, I still had hope. This wasn't the first time for me to be in such a hopeless situation. Many times when pushed against the wall, and there was no escape, the hope that I felt inside myself, helped me to get out of situations as difficult as this one. But this conversation was very hard on me. Suddenly, there was no job that I could do satisfactorily. Conversations around me and about me were not as they used to be. They were in the past tense. "Joe used to work at this job. Those were Joe's tools. Joe started this, etc., etc." I know the boys were trying to be helpful, out of respect, and this hurt even more. I wasn't around anymore, and of course, my job divided among them. As in the psalms: "They divided among them my garments".

I stood there for some time feeling alone, agitated, unwanted and worthless. Nobody needed me. If I did anything, somebody would come to me and say to take it easy, to relax, and that he would do it for me. Since the pain, caused by the BCG therapy had ceased, I felt normal. Yes, I had a terminal disease. Yes, my days were numbered, but I wasn't an invalid yet. I could do all my jobs as before, and I needed that job, if for nothing else, to forget my sickness. I needed something to keep me busy. I needed no pity. I needed some normal relationships, as if nothing had happened. Death was close. Yes, it could happen any time, but I could live a very long time too. I didn't want time to think about it. Any simple thought about anything was worse than the sickness itself; but what could it be and whom could I tell?

Dragica Donia worked on the fourth floor of my building. She was temporary office help. When we met for the first time, I recognized from her accent that we came from the same country. We became good friends, and sometimes exchanged conversation. I didn't know where to turn, so I decided to see her. I needed to talk to somebody who understood my mother tongue, to somebody who would understand me the best. She seemed the best person for that. I told her what the doctor had found. I didn't

Josip Gabre

mention the fact that the tumour was malignant. It wasn't necessary because she knew many things about cancer. She was very health conscious and had read many articles on cancer. She understood my problem right away, and didn't pity me.

"You are a strong Dalmatian. Look at yourself. You will pull yourself through this, don't worry", she said, and no doubt, she believed what she said.

I believed her too. I don't know why, but I strongly believed that I would pull through. It is necessary to mention how shaky and unrealistic my faith was. The very decision, which I had made, didn't promise me much. I know that most in a similar situation would have said yes, for when one accepts some kind of therapy, there is at least a ray of hope, despite how weak it is. In this way, what hope did I have? None! The way she observed me, the way she spoke and her opinions on this matter, shone radiantly with confidence. I believed her. I didn't know how it would happen, but her voice and her looks, full of confidence, encouraged me to fight to the last breath. I told her about the decision I had reached to refuse chemotherapy treatment.

"You made the right decision," she said.

"Do you really think so?"

"Yes, of course. At home, I have something that will help you. You will see."

"What is that?" I was burning with impatience.

"Some people cured themselves of cancer by simpler means than those offered by medicine."

She promised to show me an article written by a medical doctor who had cancer and cured himself with a macrobiotic diet. This conversation gave me courage and helped me to relax. I went back to work, and started to do my job, not worried about what my colleagues were saying. I asked them to behave as though nothing had happened, and only in this way would they be of any help to me. I decided to work harder than ever and to continue to do so as long as my health allowed. I had to be active on the job, at home, in the community, and wherever I happened to be; because when busy, I knew, I wouldn't think about my disease. That same day in St. Mary's drugstore, I bought all the needed herbs recommended by Maria Treben. The next day Dragica brought the article written by Doctor Antony Sattilaro. I share this article in its entirety in Chapter III.

CHAPTER THREE

PHYSICIAN, HEAL THYSELF

A doctor's remarkable recovery from cancer and the diet he's convinced was responsible for it.

By Dr. Antony Sattilaro and Tom Monte.

A panel of medical experts convened by the National Academy of Science issued a major report on the link between diet and cancer. The report concluded, "It is not now possible, and may never be possible, to specify a diet that would protect everyone against all forms of cancer. Nevertheless, the committee believes that it is possible...to formulate interim dietary guidelines that are both consistent with good nutritional practices and likely to reduce the risk of cancer." The report advised eating fewer saturated and unsaturated fats, salt-cured, pickled and smoked foods, and eating more vegetables, fruits and whole-grains cereals. Said the chairman of the committee: "It is time to further spread the message that cancer is not as inevitable as death and taxes."

One physician who would agree is Dr. Antony Sattilaro, president of Methodist Hospital in Philadelphia, who believes he cured his own cancer with diet, exercise and faith. His story follows.

As I had every morning for the past two years, I woke up on May 23 1978, with a dull pain in my back. I swallowed a couple of painkillers, showered, shaved and dressed, and wheeled my bicycle into the elevator of my apartment building near Rittenhouse Square. Recently I had begun bicycling to the Union League for breakfast and then to work. The traffic that morning seemed particularly thick. As I approached an intersection, a man suddenly darted in front of me; I swerved to avoid him and drove my bike into a gaping pothole. The palms of my hands and my groin took the full impact of the fall. I got up, dusted myself off and pulled some asphalt pebbles from my palms. My right testicle was screaming with pain, but I managed to bicycle the rest of the way to work.

When I arrived at the hospital, with my back and groin still hurting, I made an appointment with the radiology department. A few days later, I had X-rays and blood and liver tests taken, and returned to my office to begin the day's work. Only six months into my job as head of Methodist Hospital (I had been chairman of the anesthesiology department for 13 years), I was facing my first real test: a major inspection of the hospital's facilities, policies and staff by the Pennsylvania Department of Health. It was that inspection and not my own physical examination that I was worrying about when the phone rang. The chairman of the radiology department, Dr. Antony Renzi, was on the line.

"Tony, how do you feel?" Renzi asked.

"I feel fine," I said. "What is up?"

"Well, there is something abnormal about your chest X-ray," said Renzi. "Why don't you come down and have a look?"

When I arrived, Tony Renzi put my chest X-ray on the lighted view box, and I saw a large mass in the left side of my chest. Renzi and I discussed the X-rays, and as we did, I became strangely aware of my left lung. My breathing had become noticeably shorter and my mouth was dry. I resisted the impulse to loosen my tie. Considering the X-rays, Renzi recommended that I have a bone scan immediately. I agreed.

Within an hour I was back in radiology, where Renzi and his assistant injected a radioactive dye into my veins. I then had to wait three hours for the dye to spread throughout my body, after which a machine similar to a Geiger counter was suspended above me to detect how the dye reacted in my body. In the person with cancer, the dye collects in large quantities wherever there is cancerous tissue. When the bone scanner is held over an area of the body where the dye has collected, the machine sends out a loud and rapid clicking sound. In a person free of any tumours, the dye spreads homogeneously throughout the body and the machine clicks out a low, monotonous beat.

I lay down on the narrow table beneath the scanner; except for the hospital gown, I was naked. I was also cold and terribly nervous; my body shivered as if I were lying on a block of ice. I looked up at the machinery suspended above me. The sensitive end of the bone scanner, about the size and shape of a snare drum, attached to a computer that analyses the data. Built into the computer is an oscilloscope, or monitor, which provides an X-ray like picture of the patient. Tumours appear on the monitor as black patches; in a healthy person, the monitor shows a clear outline of the body. I cast some feeble thoughts towards heaven, making deals with the Almighty. Just before Renzi turned on the machine, I reminded myself - in an effort to steady my nerves - that doctors don't get sick.

Renzi threw the switch on the bone scanner, and like some massive creature that had just been awakened, it responded with a slow, desultory clicking sound, apparently picking up stray radioactive particles in the air. The scanner's sensory drum was placed over my head, and suddenly the clicking sound shifted from a low, sporadic beat to a wild and terrifying machine-gun fire. My heart seemed to be keeping pace with it. My skin was suddenly galvanized by a wave of adrenaline and body heat. I took a quick look over at the monitor and saw to my disbelief what looked like a black spot at the top of my head. Renzi moved the machine down to my right shoulder, and after a brief pause in the clicking, the manic beat started again. It was the same over my sternum, my back and the left side of my rib cage. I withdrew into a state of shock, but the sound of the click followed me inwards. It was as if the clicking sounds were taking place deep within the centre of my brain. They were cancer cells made audible.

I got up from the table and wanted to vomit. Somehow my stomach held on while Renzi and I went over the test results. According to the bone scan, I had cancerous lesions in my skull, my left sixth rib, my right shoulder, and my sternum and back. Later, Renzi came down to my office and tried to console me. He appeared stiff, as if he wanted to exhale a long breath but couldn't.

"Tony, really, I don't think we can make any conclusions based on the bone scan," he said to me. "There is a chance it could have been reacting to some benign activity in the bone tissue. We really won't know for sure until you have a biopsy. Please, let's not jump to any conclusions until we know for sure. O.K. Tony?"

"O.K." I mumbled. I could barely hear my own voice through the distant drone of clicking still going off in my mind.

The following morning I took all my test results to my physician, Dr. Sheldon Lisker. An internist and oncologist - a doctor who specializes in the diagnosis and treatment of tumours - Dr.

Lisker had been my physician and friend since the late 1960s. He examined me, paying particular attention to the swollen right testicle, which by now was abnormally hard. We then sat and discussed the tests together. He told me that my blood tests had revealed that my phosphatase levels were sharply elevated, showing the possibility of cancer. My liver function tests were also abnormal, continuing a pattern established the previous summer when I had contracted hepatitis. He then took my bone scan results, which provided X-ray like pictures, and put them on the lighted view box for examination.

"Tony," Dr. Lisker said. "After looking at all of this, I have to tell you that I think you have either a testicular or prostatic carcinoma. There is a good chance that the cancer has spread to the other parts of your body as showen by the bone scan. I think you should have that testicle biopsied immediately. We should also have a biopsy done on the prostate gland."

Dr. Lisker and I discussed the possibilities further. There were a couple of incongruities in my case that did not fit into the classic pattern for either prostatic or testicular cancer. The latter usually do not spread to the bone, whereas my bone scan clearly indicated some type of bone lesion. On the other hand, prostatic cancer does not often afflict Caucasian men in my age group. I was 46. White males usually do not contract cancer of the prostate until they are 50 and over. Prostatic cancer in men under 50 is much different, and a far more perilous disease than for older men, often killing its victims within two or three years after diagnosis. Lisker tried to console me, but both of us knew that if the biopsy proved positive, I probably wouldn't see my fiftieth birthday.

Sheldon Lisker's office is very near my home. When I left him, I walked to Rittenhouse Square. It was the 1st June, a warm and elegant spring day. The park benches were occupied by people eating their lunches in the shadows of the tall trees. Perfect sailing weather, I thought. An artist was displaying his work in one corner of the square. I browsed through his collection and spotted an oil painting of two tennis players that I immediately wanted to buy. I was about to ask the artist the price when, suddenly, the thought that I was trying desperately to repress, spilled over the walls of my consciousness. You're going to die, my mind cried out. What's the point? I turned on my heel and hurried home.

That afternoon I called Dr. John Prehatny, the chairman of our department of surgery, to arrange to have the testicle and prostate glands biopsied. I would have to have the testicle removed. John and I agreed to do the operation on Tuesday. I then arranged to check into Methodist as a patient on Monday.

Over the weekend I drove to Long Beach Island, NJ, to rest at my summer home and visit my parents, who lived nearby. Ironically, my father had been dying of cancer for the previous six months, and I did not dare tell my mother that I now had cancer. Instead of telling her I was checking into the hospital, I said I would be gone for two weeks on a business trip and would call when I returned.

The following week I was operated on, by my own hospital staff. My right testicle and all the lymph nodes on the right side of my groin were removed, and a transrectal biopsy was done on the prostate itself. When the result came back, they showed that the prostate was filled with cancer. The next step was clear. My left sixth rib would have to be removed to see if the cancer had spread to the areas shown by the scan. The only way to know was to surgically remove the rib and examine it.

On June 13th, the day after my 47th birthday, the rib was removed, and a tumour the size of a plum was discovered growing out of it. The rib and tumour were sent down to the pathology lab to check for malignancy. If the tumour turned out to be benign, there was a chance that the machine had reacted to benign bone tissue activity, and that the cancer, localized in the prostate glands, could be treated with surgery. The results from the lab would be crucial.

It was almost a week later when Dr. Prehatny, my surgeon, came into my hospital room and sat on the end of the bed. Before he spoke, he just looked at me, perhaps to give me a chance to read the bad news on his face.

"I've got many problems telling you this Tony," John said. "But the rib is loaded with cancer." The operation confirmed the diagnosis: prostatic cancer stage IV (D). I knew that I had between 18 months and three years to live.

"I am disappointed, John," I said. I couldn't stop the tears from coming.

Prehatny paused and added, "I've talked to Dr. Lisker, Tony, and he agrees that we should take off the other testicle."

The following morning I went up to the operating room for the third time in three weeks. The surgery - called an orchiectomy - required about an hour. I was back in my room by eleven. The anaesthetic wore off around noon. For a while I sat in bed thinking. I was no longer whole. I felt less than a human. What was I anymore? I knew what I was. I just sat there and sobbed. I was losing my life in great chunks. A rush of shock and anger filled my stomach and swelled into my chest.

"No, dear God, no..." I cried.

I made it through the summer mostly on Percodan, a narcotic pain reliever. I had gone into the hospital for the relief of pain, but the pain was worse now than ever. Everything I did was governed by it. I took a couple of Percodan tablets every six hours, and the combination of pain relief and narcotic stimulation drove me to euphoric heights. Magically my problems seemed to fit into small boxes in my mind; my life became manageable. But of course the euphoria did not last. After a couple of hours the Percodan would wear off, and I would swing back towards the other end of the spectrum. I became deeply depressed. These symptoms were all to familiar. I had watched my father follow the same pattern in his slow and unmerciful slide towards death.

On the last day of July my father began having brain seizures. He needed extensive medical attention, and my mother and I decided to bring him to Methodist Hospital. That day I told my mother that I, too, had cancer.

"It was local and removed. Don't worry," I told her.

"Isn't that what we said about your father's disease? Local. Don't worry," my mother said.

A little later she added, " your father knew all the while."

"Knew what?"

"Your father knew you had cancer. He told me after we saw you the last time. He said, 'Tony's got it too.' He just shook his head and kept saying that - 'Tony's got it too'."

The sick and the dying recognize one another, I thought to myself.

On the 7th of August my father died. On the 9th th August we held a funeral mass at St. Francis Church on Long Beach Island. The following day we buried him in the family plot in Hopelawn, NJ. It was a hot and humid afternoon, and I was very depressed. My cancer did not seem to be in remission, my pain was worse than ever, and in attending my father's funeral, I almost felt as if I had attended my own.

As I drove back to Philadelphia I noticed two hitchhikers on the side of the road, both in their early twenties, with hair down over their ears and wearing jeans and sport shirts. Normally, I would have passed them by. I had a prejudice against young people with long hair and their attacks against the establishment, particularly because it was my own profession that was often being criticized. But this day, for a reason I do not understand, I picked them up. Little did I realize how important these two young men would turn out to be in my life.

Sean McLean sat with me in the front seat while Bill Bochbracher stretched out on the back seat and fell asleep. McLean and I began talking. Both men, it turned out, had just graduated from a natural foods cooking program sponsored by the Seventh Inn Restaurant in Boston. When the conversation got around to me, I told McLean that I had just buried my father, and that I, too, was dying of cancer.

My companion shot back in an almost cavalier fashion. "You know, you don't have to die, Doc. Cancer isn't all that hard to cure." I looked at him as if he were just a silly kid. What does a twenty-five-year-old cook know about cancer, I thought? I dismissed what he said as a foolishness of youth.

"Actually, Sean, cancer is very hard to cure," I informed him. "About four hundred thousand Americans die of it each year. It's the second leading killer disease in the US. There are no easy answers, believe me."

"Listen, cancer is the natural result of bad diet," McLean responded. "When you eat lots of red meat, lots of dairy products, eggs, refined foods, like sugar and white flour, and foods high in chemical preservatives, then you get cancer. That is if you don't die of a heart attack first. Diet causes cancer," he said confidently. "But you can reverse the disease by changing your diet to one of whole grains and vegetables. People have already done it. And you can do it too."

I forgot the advice of my passenger almost as soon as he got out of my car. After twenty years of practicing medicine, I had heard all kinds of quack claims; I dismissed what McLean had said as nonsense.

Days later, returning to my apartment with raging back pain, I was handed a pink postal slip by the security guard, telling me that a package was waiting in the mail room with 67 cents postage due. It was from Sean McLean. Inside I found a booklet titled *A Macrobiotic Approach to Cancer*. Macrobiotics? Isn't that the crazy brown rice diet, I thought? I went into the den, lay uncomfortably on the couch and paged through the booklet.

A Macrobiotic Approach to Cancer was basically a booklet of testimonials from people who claimed that macrobiotics had cured them of cancer, which in many cases had been diagnosed as terminal by medical doctors. I gave it a rather cursory perusal and was about to toss the thing into the wastebasket when I spotted the name of Dr. Ruth Schaefer, whose testimonial described her successful treatment of breast cancer with macrobiotics. Her statement went on to say that she was a practicing physician in Philadelphia. I put the booklet down, looked up Ruth Schaefer's name in the medical directory and decided to call. A man answered the telephone.

"Hello," I said. "Is Dr.Ruth Schaefer in?"

"Do you know my wife?" asked Mr. Schaefer.

"No, I don't. I was just reading a testimonial she gave in the booklet *A macrobiotic approach to Cancer*, and I was wondering if I might speak to her about it."

"I'm sorry," he said. "My wife isn't here. She's in the hospital dying of cancer."

"Oh, I see. Well, you've answered my question. Macrobiotics doesn't cure cancer." I was about to hang up when Mr. Schaefer came back enthusiastically.

Josip Gabre

"Listen," he said. "It really works. While she was sticking to the diet, it really did help her. She showed real signs of getting well. But she couldn't stick to it. She hated the food."

"Do you think it's worth looking into? I'm dying of cancer," I said.

"Yes, definitely," was Mr. Schaefer's answer. He then gave me the telephone number of Denny Waxman, the director of the Philadelphia East West Foundation, an educational organization for macrobiotics.

I called Denny Waxman, and in so doing entered the alien world of macrobiotics. For the next seven months, I ate at the Waxmans' table, sharing their food and listened to the macrobiotic philosophy. Because my condition was so serious, Denny Waxman and his wife Judy imposed the strictest diet possible. All the food that I was accustomed to, and fondest of, was out: all meat, dairy products, refined grains, including white bread and flour products, all sugar, oils, nuts, fruits, carbonated beverages, and food containing synthetic chemicals and preservatives. Alcohol was also taboo. I was placed on a diet consisting of 50 to 60 percent whole grains, especially brown rice; 25 percent locally grown, cooked vegetables; 15 percent beans and sea vegetables; and the rest, soup and condiments.

I was certain I was turning myself over to a band of quacks. I realized I was desperate and therefore vulnerable. In the end, however, I had no alternative. It was either, do something different, or die. And one thing was for sure. It was different. At the Waxmans' table, food was shared with several other macrobiotic enthusiasts. I listened incredulously to the macrobiotic philosophy of cancer. The diseases I understood from my own training, which was of infinite complexity - were reduced to a simple metaphor, one that revolved around the theory of balance.

My shallow hope that a macrobiotic diet was an answer to cancer was diminishing in stages, as Denny Waxman delved deeper into the macrobiotic theory. He began with the history of the American diet, arguing that since the early part of the century, our diet had steadily degenerated. In 1900 Americans ate mostly whole grains, fresh vegetables and fruit, with a much smaller proportion of red meat, dairy products, artificial colouring and preservatives. The diet then was concentrated around complex carbohydrates, particularly those derived from whole wheat, potatoes, barley, oats and rice.

With the rise of technology in the 20th century came the much more synthetic diets of today. Most of our food is heavily processed. Vegetables are generally an accessory to the principal food, which is meat. The American diet is now centred around animal products to the extent that about 40 percent of our calories consist of fat, most of it saturated animal fat. Refined grains and packaged vegetables, sugar and artificial chemicals make up the rest of the regimens.

At the same time we have witnessed an incredible rise in the incidence of certain degenerative diseases, particularly cardiovascular disease and cancer. Waxman claimed that the increase in these illnesses is due largely to the degeneration of the American diet. In countries where a diet similar to macrobiotics is eaten, he pointed out, there is an extremely low incidence of heart disease and cancer.

The macrobiotic view is that this degeneration can be reversed through sound dietary habits and a healthy lifestyle. Waxman maintained that cancer is the result of an extreme imbalance in the body, due largely to unhealthy eating. Balance can be restored by eating food that allows the body to naturally discharge the toxins (i.e. fat, refined and synthetic products, chemicals, etc.) from the system.

I had a real problem accepting Denny's argument. To suggest that diet was the root cause of cancer seemed an incredible oversimplification of the etiology of this disease. Waxman's line of reasoning did not take into account several other possible causes of cancer, including genetic predisposition, viruses or carcinogens in the environment. In the last analysis, macrobiotics was a faith system and one that I had little faith in. I could not accept that these people - most of whom had no medical or scientific training - could have an answer to the problem that has baffled the most brilliant minds in the country.

Yet I knew I would continue to eat at the Waxmans'. I had no other alternative. When you are dying you become desperate, and your prejudices and pride become luxuries you can no longer afford. I would not give up the standard treatment I was receiving (daily doses of the female hormone estrogen), but I was forced to try for a long shot. Macrobiotics was the only one presented to me.

So every night that September I went back to the Waxmans' house for dinner. Judy Waxman made enough for me to take for lunch the following day, and I made my own breakfast of miso soup and oatmeal. I was back working at the hospital full time now. Each day I carried to the office my little Japanese lunch box containing brown rice and vegetables. People at the hospital looked at me with a combination of curiosity and pity. There was even a strange disappointment in their eyes, as if I had gone to the other side. "He's turned himself over to the quacks," many of them must have thought. I would have thought the same thing had a colleague of mine resorted to macrobiotics in his dying days.

The pain was with me as great as ever. I had also gained considerable weight as a result of the estrogen. Within weeks after I began the treatments, I went from 140 pounds to 170, much of it water retention. I was bloated and my skin itched profusely. As a distraction, I threw myself into planning the hospital's building program - and into macrobiotics.

The diet and philosophy were actually becoming exciting for me in the way that any new course of study had been in my past. I became the student again at the Waxmans' table.

During the first weeks, there were few subtle signs that suggested my condition might be changing. Then something dramatic happened. On the 26 of September 1978, a Tuesday, I woke up at my usual hour of 6:30. Still sleepy, I reached over to the night table for my bottle of Percodan. It was a Pavlovian reaction. Suddenly I was struck by an overwhelming perception. The back pain was gone. Completely disappeared. I got out of bed and walked around the apartment searching my back with my mind. There was no doubt about it; the pain was gone. I didn't know what to make of it. After two years of suffering with enormous back pain that only heavy doses of narcotics could put down, I was suddenly free of pain. It was like being released from a straitjacket. As soon as I reached my office, I called Denny Waxman and told him the news. I asked him if he thought the diet was responsible.

"It's the diet, Tony. And it's a great sign," Waxman said. "You're doing wonderfully."

In the weeks that followed, however, my elation at being relieved of the pain turned into feelings of loneliness and despair. By late October, my spirit had fallen with the leaves. I had two strikes against me: I had cancer and I was practicing macrobiotics. The cancer alone was enough to make people uncomfortable around me. They were either incredibly solicitous or so distant that it made me wonder if they didn't believe cancer was infectious.

Macrobiotics only complicated the matter. I no longer went out to dinner with friends and colleagues. When I had to attend a professional affair where food was being served, I brought my own. While everyone else was cutting into their filet mignon, I'd be opening my Japanese lunch box and removing a rice ball and some vegetables. Most of my colleagues regarded me with patronizing curiosity: "Gee, Tony, that is interesting." Others observed at tense and dignified distance; they simply didn't speak to me.

Of course, I understood their feelings. Generally, physicians regard alternative health approaches as a charlatanism and a fraud against the public. By indulging in an alternative approach myself, I was seen as lending credence to a system that could be dangerous to the patients.

Despite these emotional trials I was becoming increasingly convinced that this crazy diet was making me feel better physically than I had felt in years. For the previous 20 years I suffered from chronic intestinal problems. I had been taking a variety of medications, all of which proved virtually useless. However, within weeks after I began the macrobiotic diet, my digestive problems disappeared. On top of that, I had great reserves of energy and my mind seemed clearer than usual. At first I attributed this increased vitality and mental clarity to my recovery from surgery. However, as time wore on and I continued to feel improvement, I decided that the diet was at least partly responsible; I did not remember feeling this well before the surgery - or before the back pain, for that matter.

On the 22nd of January 1979, I had a blood and liver function test at Methodist. The following day the results were delivered to Dr. Sheldon Lisker, who went over them with me. Seven months before, on the 31st of May 1978, my blood and liver function studies had indicated the presence of cancer. The alkaline phosphatase level in my blood was 69; the normal was between 9 and 35. My SGOT and SGPT, both liver function tests and both key indicators of cancer, were 100 and 273, respectively. The normal range for both tests is between 13 and 40.

On the 23rd of January however, I was told of some notable changes. My alkaline phosphatase level had dropped to 36; the SGOT had dropped to 21 and my SGPT had gone down to 27. My condition had improved dramatically.

Dr. Lisker attributed the improvement to the orchiectomy and the estrogen treatment. He said that these were good signs and admitted that they were somewhat out of the ordinary. But he was cautious in his interpretation of the test results. They did not mean that the cancer was eliminated, he said, or even in the process of remission. It simply meant that the disease might have been temporarily arrested. Nevertheless, I was encouraged. I had read the studies on my type of carcinoma, and my pattern seemed unique. When Sheldon and I finished going over the tests, I very cautiously asked him if he thought my diet was in any way responsible for my improvement.

"No, Tony. There is no scientific evidence that I'm aware of which suggests diet plays any role in the treatment of cancer. At least not the kind of role you're talking about."

"Well, there may not be any evidence to support the hypothesis, Sheldon, but I'm beginning to believe that this diet is helping me," I said. "I don't know how it's doing it, but I feel much better, beyond what you might attribute to the recovery from surgery.

In June 1979 I drove to Phoenixville PA, for my second examination by Michio Kushi, the founder of the East West foundation, and the Erewhon natural food business, the author of several books on traditional Oriental medicine and the leading proponent of macrobiotics in the United States.

Just as traditional healers have done for centuries, Kushi used Oriental diagnostic techniques to ascertain the state of patients' health. By closely examining the face, eyes, feet and other areas of the body, Kushi was said to be able to assess a person's health with impressive accuracy. After probing various areas of my body with his thumb and issuing a few low groans, Kushi stood back and looked at me in the way we do when we want to remember someone's face.

"You don't have cancer anymore Tony. You have beaten your disease."

Suddenly a wall of tension, desperation, pain and disappointment collapsed; joy rushed through me like healing waters. I asked Kushi when he believed I could successfully undergo a bone scan. I wanted to have scientific proof that I had beaten the cancer.

"The test is dangerous, Tony," Kushi said. "You know that radioactive dye is not on the macrobiotic diet." Kushi advised me to wait until December.

"I've got to know for sure," I said. "And the test is the only way to do that."

In light of my lingering skepticism about the macrobiotic approach, I decided to test the diet; in the middle of June, 1979, I discontinued the estrogens entirely. I was never to resume taking the hormones. I also scheduled a bone scan for the 27th of September.

That early fall morning, driving to the office, I prayed like a man on his way to the gallows. When I arrived at the hospital, I went down to the X-ray department, where Dr. Renzi injected the radioactive dye into my veins. As we waited the three hours for the dye to spread throughout my system, Renzi came to my office and told me what he expected to find from the bone scan. Referring to my blood and liver tests, he said, "You've arrested the disease, Tony," adding that my X-rays would show no progression of the lesion, and that was "a very good sign." However, Renzi admonished me not to be disappointed when we found the disease in the same basic pattern that it had displayed on the 31st of May 1978. "Bones take a long time to heal, Tony. They're very deep and we can't expect much change over fifteen months." Renzi got out of his chair and smiled. "See you in a couple of hours." As soon as I returned to the radiology department and lay down on the table I became terribly nervous. I looked at the bone scanner. Some irrational fears of the machine came over me. It was coldly objective. There was nothing forgiving in that machine. I knew it would search like a wild blood hound until it ferreted out a tumour in me. Yet, I was hopeful. I remembered Kushi's diagnosis.

Renzi turned on the machine, and immediately it began clicking out a slow, monotonous beat. When he brought the drum down over my head the beat picked up, responding to the radioactive dye in my body. However, it remained steady and normal. I looked over at the oscilloscope and saw the X-ray- like outline of my head; there was no black patch as there had been 15 months before. There was no tumour in my scull! Renzi manipulated the sensitive end of the machine from my head to my shoulder; again, there was no change in the beat of the clicks, and again no black patch in the oscilloscope. My shoulder was healed! Renzi moved the drum over my entire body from head to foot. He made careful passes over the areas where the cancer had shown up before: the scull, right shoulder, sternum, rib cage, spine and genitals. As Renzi directed the bone scan near my heart, my mind, my entire being were rivetted on the cadence of the clicks. Every time he changed the placement of the drum, I shifted my head to see the oscilloscope.

All was normal. My bones were healed. The cancer was gone. Renzi was shocked. I got off the table and more X-rays were taken of my body. Still no sign of cancer. Renzi told me in amazement that he had never seen anything like this before.

I was overcome with joy. I gave Dr. Renzi a big bear hug. "I don't know what you're doing Tony," he said to me. "But, by God, keep doing it."

Later that afternoon I took my X-ray results over to Sheldon Lisker's office. Like Renzi, he had expected to find little change in the basic pattern of the disease.

"Tony, I'm very happy about this, though I want to caution you that we should continue to watch your progress," Lisker said. "Still, from all the tests, you're fine. I want to congratulate you." He smiled and shook my hand.

"Sheldon, what do you think caused this change in my condition?" I asked.

"Frankly, Tony, I don't know. I can only assume that it was the therapy - the orchiectomy and the estrogens - that triggered your auto immune system to fight off the cancer."

"Have you ever seen another case like mine?" I asked.

"No, I haven't," he said. "I'd say that your case is rare; I do understand that there are a few cases reported like this in the British literature. I think perhaps we might look at those cases to see what similarities there are."

"How does this affect the five-year survival rate?" I asked.

"Tony, we may as well throw those books out the window," Sheldon said. "When the bones are clean, where's the disease? We don't know what is going to happen to you from this point. That's why we've got to watch your condition."

Lisker then said that he could not advise me to go off the macrobiotic diet, or go back on the estrogens. "You seem to be flourishing on the diet," Sheldon said. "I wish you well."

In the months that followed I began a new life, filled with joy and a new faith. I now felt the need to attend Catholic mass daily. Everything charged me with elation - a pile of papers on my desk, routine interactions with others, the great rush of people coming along Broad Street. I felt renewed in body and soul.

The fall of 1980, however, brought another round of trials. In September the back pain returned; in October a bone scan revealed a small lesion in my right eighth rib. Was the cancer returning? Would I soon be riddled with tumours again? I had not been taking the estrogens for 15 months now, plenty of time for their effectiveness to wear off and for the cancer to return.

My macrobiotic associates assured me that the spot was just another discharge of toxins that would soon disappear. I fell back on the two things that had supported me through the last two years: the diet and my religious roots. Two days after Christmas, I had another bone scan. The spot had nearly disappeared, Renzi told me that the lesion was in fact regressing and was now reduced to a mere shadow. My confidence returned.

On 6 August 1981, I had yet another bone scan - the sixth in three years. The faint gray on my right side was now completely gone. There was no sign of cancer anywhere in my body. I was diagnosed by my doctors as in "complete remission".

Today I remain in the best health I've experienced in 30 years. My job as president of Methodist Hospital and my frequent lecturing on diet and cancer keep me busier than ever. I am still careful about my diet but I've widened my regimen to include fish and fruit. Once a month, I even sneak a beer.

*Dr. Sattilaro is of course describing only his own experi-
ence, and as he himself says, "Anecdotal evidence, such as my
own story is not regarded as scientific proof of anything. Oncologists remain almost totally skeptical about the claims made for
the macrobiotic diet, and point out that a patient with prostatic
cancer, among other types of the disease, must be monitored for
years before he is considered cured. Neither Dr. Sattilaro nor any
other physician would recommend that a cancer victim - or anyone else - remain without careful consultation to the skim of the
diet that he himself followed. He believes that case histories like
this will stimulate scientific research and perhaps new ideas that
may eventually lead to a more effective treatment and a cure for
this disease.*

After reading this article I was astounded and appalled simultaneously. Doctor medicine! ? He says openly how medicine
and the methods it uses were crippling him, and how his body was
cut to pieces without any results. Yet his colleagues remain skeptical although the results are quite clear. They know exactly what
methods were used, but still they deny the possibility that something other than their treatments caused his recovery. Why is it
so? I was absorbed in thought. Isn't the same thing happening to
me too? Now I had no doubt that my decision to refuse therapy,
recommended by my physician, was the right one. Through this
article the whole truth was revealed to me. I knew by now that I
couldn't expect help from modern medicine, because, for one reason or another it couldn't give me it. What now? There was nothing and nobody I could turn to. Where could I find the macrobiotic food that Dr. Sattilaro was talking about? In Toronto then
there was no such thing. I faded slowly towards death.

NOTE: When this translation was ready I sent one copy of
this manuscript to Mr. Wayne Martin, former editor of American
Cancer Magazine. To the Sattilaro story this is his reply.

"The story of the doctor with prostate cancer does not ring true. For the past 50 years surgical castration and later medical castration with estrogen has been standard practice in treating prostate cancer. In the practice of castration, it has been surgical OR medical castration, not surgical AND medical castration. If the doctor had surgical castration there was no need to give him estrogen. Both surgical and medical castrations often lead to a quick remission of prostate cancer. There are two papers in The Lancet, one for the 4th of August 1984 page 281-2 and the other for the 29th of June 1985 page 1507 in which after medical castration, quick remissions occurred. One of these patients had a lung metastasis from a prostate carcinoma and the other had both, lung and bone metastasis. The one with the bone metastasis had a striking relief from bone pain in four weeks time.

In these cases, medical castration was achieved not with estrogen, but with an LHRH analogue. Results just as good could have been obtained with surgical castration.

What is wrong with both medical and surgical castration is that the remissions are most often of short duration, however in your report we see a group of doctors acting like they did not expect a remission after surgical castration when what could be expected was the remission that did take place. So what is wrong with this story until now is that surgical castration and estrogen should not be needed together and the kind of remission described was to be expected as the result of castration.

Now, if the patient stayed on the macrobiotic diet and lived in remission for many years, then something new had been added. Remission from surgical and medical castration most often does not last more than three years. However, often the kinds of remission described in your MS are to be expected because of either medical or surgical castration.

39   *Josip Gabre*

You have this one, lasting two years. This is well within the scope of remission caused by surgical castration.

Truly, Dr. Sattilaro is now dead. I to date have no further information regarding how long he lived after remission occured, as per the conditions Mr. Martin described.

Is it any wonder why Dr. Sattilaro felt alineated from his profession while trying to heal himself?

I believe this is a classic case of how difficult it is to serve two masters.

A SPECIAL NOTE TO READERS OF THIS 3RD EDITION

Many people ask me about nutrition. What to eat? This is the hardest question to answer these days. How important good and right nutrition is, goes beyond our comprehension. What can we say about that? Several years ago I considered writing a book on this subject, but when I read the works of several authors, I found that none of them agreed about anything on the subject. Then who was I, to shed even more confusion?

Let us earnestly study our body to find what is happening inside it. What is our cell, what function does it perform, how does it behave and so on? As microscopic as our cell is, it is the replica of our being. She needs proteins, minerals, vitamins and enzymes in *natural basics*, and of course oxygen. She needs a normal peaceful life without stress and strain, because she needs to do a very important job. As we are polluting everything around ourselves, we do the same within ourselves too. Feeding our cells with anything but, as I already said, proteins, vitamins, minerals and enzymes we cause stress within ourselves, and we weaken our cells. In such a condition they are either dying peacefully or they are rebelling. Considering, what cancer is, how it appears, behaves and so on, we already have all the answers we need. I emphasized, *natural basics* which is very important, because it is only natural food or medicine that we can easily assimilate and eliminate. Synthetics in contrast, we cannot readily, assimilate or

Josip Gabre

eliminate at all. Therefore, the residuals accumulate within our body creating a burden on our cells and in turn we get sick. Let us look around; don't we do the same thing within our society? Today, where can we get needed ingredients in our food? Mostly everything that we consume here have chemicals added, and are consequently dead nutritionally, which amounts to our problem. More dead food, more residuals, less nourishment, less strength, less vitality, less happiness and so on.

Therefore, what to eat? From biblical times we learned that certain food, for somebody is poison and for somebody else is medicine. We easily fall for professionally described types of food, therefore, from there we learn that we are either vegetarian or meat eaters.

Christa Giessen N.M.N.D.,D.B.M.,C.H wrote a booklet by the title WHY MOST DIETS DON'T WORK. Reading that booklet I was forced to change my opinion about our diet. She said: *"All human blood may be divided into four main types or groups; O, A, B, and AB."* According to her, blood group O or B are the meat eaters and A and AB the vegetarians. To me it makes sense. But, let's go back to the ingredients that our cells require. As we just said our cell is the replica of our being, therefore let us not separate those two facts.

According to what we just said, any food depleted from: Natural proteins, vitamins, minerals and enzymes are actually dead food, and we cannot nourish ourselves with it. Therefore I don't see the reason to restrict ourselves from different kinds of food before we solve the main problem, chemicals. Therefore, before we do anything else, we have to choose foods without chemicals. We have to avoid: Sugar and white bread, because they are bleached, meaning everything good in them which gives us taste or nourishment is taken from it, and chemicals added to make them consumable. All processed food has to be avoided, or any other where chemicals are suspected to be added.

For proper elimination food with lots of fibre has to be eaten as it helps us to eliminate properly. Therefore, salads and sprouts are extremely good. Sprouts can be home grown and they are the best. Any healthfood store can give us information how to do it.

I get many questions from people about microwave ovens. Do I have to spell it out again? In microwave ovens, food is cooked from the inside out. Does any heat or natural way of cooking do that? What is it? I call it radiation, regardless of somebody disagreeing with me or not. Is radiation harmful? Do I have to spell it out too? Besides, any food prepared that way, despite radiation, is dead food. Microwaves destroy anything nutrient in that food. Many say "We just reheat stuff with it." That is the double error. Any reheat destroys enzymes and vitamins, left in the food, and reheating it in the microwave oven is even worse. Therefore, these mothers who prepare or reheat even milk in the microwave oven are doing a disservice to their infants, and are preparing them for all kinds of possible diseases in their later lives.

In conclusion I would say, any food without chemicals, where nutrients are saved, is good food, regardless, of their being vegetarian.

Many times I hear: "Cancer feeds from such and such food..." Cancer feeds from any food and I don't see how it feeds more from one and less from another. We damaged our cell population with dead, chemically filled food, namely we poison ourselves with chemicals and therein lies our problem.

CHAPTER FOUR

(STRESSING THE POINT)

Innumerable times I contemplated, how did I get this disease? I believed that if I discovered the reason, more than likely I could deal with it. Going back to the theory of corrupting our system with food, drink, air, water pollution, and other things, referred by doctors Cameron and Pauling, I knew that these were not the culprits. I lived a very orderly and healthy life. In my home we ate only natural, healthy and fresh food. I drank one glass of homemade wine with my meals, in which there were no additives. I never drank other alcoholic beverages. I quit smoking twenty-eight years ago, and avoided smokey places. Although, as Mr. Wayne Martin mentioned in his note that smoking is causing bladder cancer, I don't know if that can happen after so long an absence from it. Even if the true cause for the cancer existed for such a long time, dormant, waiting for occasion to be triggered; what else could be considered that triggered the cancer occurrence? I didn't take any drugs, so, that possibility was excluded too. One more factor remained, and that was stress. When I considered it more closely, I realized that stress caused all my problems.

Three years earlier I had lost my business, and with it alot of money. I had to declare bankruptcy, otherwise the creditors would have taken the shirt off my back. Around me everything was falling apart, and there was the possibility that I would lose my family too. My family was all I had then. I was so depressed that I felt pain in my chest. One, who hasn't experienced something similar could not possibly believe or understand it. I tried to get out of this situation but on the contrary, I was getting deeper and deeper into trouble. I was running into the people who tried to use my situation to their advantage and this led to more trouble.

With no way out, and in need of work, I phoned Mr. Burt Hoggings, my former supervisor at the Ministry of the Environment in the Ontario Government. Then, he was the personnel referent for the Air Resources branch. I got the job right away, because they needed someone with my qualifications and experience. He had been looking for me for a long time, but my telephone number wasn't listed. Hope overwhelmed me, and again, I could see a rosy future ahead. At my age, (then I was 56 years old), it wasn't easy to find a job. I put my heart and soul into it to show my appreciation.

In the begining my work was very much praised. My junior supervisor used to say that he needed noone else besides me. For some unknown reason the situation changed overnight, and whatever work I had done was no longer adequate. It is not necessary to go into detail on how and why it happened, only, what caused it to happen. There was a possibility that I would lose my job, and intentions were as such. Others, who obtained their positions simultaneously as I did, were taken off from probation and given permanent positions. My probation was extended for six months. This had never happened before, but I was an exception.

After my probation had been extended, I wasn't myself anymore. All my previous capabilities vanished. Whatever I did, I was convinced that I would fail, or that somebody wouldn't like the way I had done it. As such, I became unworthy of any job. This affected my nervous system, and if I hadn't gotten cancer, I possibly would have had a nervous breakdown, or something else. I am diabetic, and had problems concentrating. I believe my sugar level at the time was very high. Rumour had it, that I was on drugs or was drinking, and when such suspicions occur, they are hard to defend against. I strongly believe that my disease was a consequence of these conditions. My immune system weakened and as such I became prone to many illnesses, including cancer.

In his book CANCER AND VITAMIN C, Dr. Pauling clearly states that we can't ask how many people contracted cancer, but rather how many were spared from the disease. In other words, cancer cells are produced by our body in great numbers, as are healthy cells, with the difference that all cancer cells are destroyed by our immune system at the very moment they are created. When our immune system fails, something drastic happens. Cancer cells multiply freely to the detriment of our system, because our immune system is not able to destroy them anymore.

I was certain that this was the cause of my illness. I understood that to cure myself from cancer I had to eliminate the problem that caused it. No cure could ever be successful if the problem wasn't understood first, leading to its eventual correction. What could I do about it? Could I try to be jovial, and forget my problems? No, I couldn't do that. Could I start drinking so that I would think no more of my situation? No, because I am of a stronger will, and am aware that if it is necessary to suffer, let it be, but not without a fight. Could I go to my senior supervisor, who was in question, and say: "Sir, please... you know, your attitude towards me bothers me so much that it is affecting my health and my job?" I couldn't do that either, because if he had been sympathetic towards me, all this wouldn't have happened. Besides, in all likelihood, the opposite effect would be achieved. Therefore I had only one choice and that was to suffer through it, and weaken more every day.

Instead of being rewarded, I was being punished in the worst possible way. Even the healthiest person in his late fifties has a hard time finding a job. What could I expect, with an incurable disease on top of that? If I lost this job, I knew I would be on the street. My director knew nothing about my situation. Several months later, I accidentally met him on the street. I told him about my situation and he was astounded and angry, because he had never been told about it. Nevertheless, the situation remained unchanged.

Perhaps my nature helped me to orientate myself in this situation. By nature I am a very open-minded person. I never hide anything from others, especially from friends. I spoke openly about my illness and never dramatized it. Through self-openness I hoped that maybe somewhere, I would find somebody who could probably help me to find a cure for my illness. Dragica Donia brought me a photocopy of the article by Dr. Sattilaro, as she had promised. I believed every word he said, but where was I to find macrobiotic food? That possibility of a cure vanished immediately. I drank the tea prescribed by Maria Treben and waited. Waited for what? Death, of course.

On Monday October the 10th I was admitted to the Hospital. The next day I was taken to the operating room, where my Dr. urologist would clean my bladder. When I awakened from the anaesthesia, he came to my bedside and told me that he never touched my bladder and that he could have hurt me even more if he had. He confirmed earlier cystoscopic findings that my bladder was all covered with cancer. He recommended surgery again but

I categorically refused it. He told me again that it was just a matter of time before I would bleed, and that would be my end. Nevertheless, I didn't consent to it.

Everything, that had been done so far brought me to this much more difficult situation. Nobody could convince me that the BCG therapy could help me in any way. Therefore I was skeptical about anything my physician suggested to me again.

CHAPTER FIVE

(DECIDING NOT TO DECIDE)

While searching for a cancer cure at a time when my brother-in-law had it as well, I was informed about Hydrazine. From literature, I learned that research was done with it in the USA and Russia. I bought Hydrazine and sent it to my brother-in-law, but he passed away before he could receive it. A friend of mine, Mrs. Petra Fantov, who suffered from colon cancer, used it instead. Hydrazine helped her, and from the beginning she felt much, much better. The pain soon disappeared. However I soon learned, that Hydrazine destroys good cells and also cancer cells. It was no different from chemotherapy or any other therapy used by medical science. I couldn't accept this therapy because the results were the same: destruction of both cancer and healthy cells as well and with the same end result... early death.

It is possible that Hydrazine isn't as harmful as chemotherapy, where toxins such as: 2-chloroethyl sulfide, was used. This toxin, also called "mustard gas", was used on the battlefield during World War I. After having read more on Hydrazine, I understood the effect it had on her and the reason for the disappearance of the pain. Regardless, I couldn't decide to take it. Why? The answer is: If it cannot cure me, why bother? Better to die as soon as possible without much suffering. Even though I knew that many people's lives were prolonged with it for several years, I couldn't make the decision to use it. I couldn't accept it, like I couldn't accept chemotherapy and its destruction of healthy cells and also cancer cells. I was very skeptical about any cure that was weakening the entire system. I decided, to take the herbal treatments, and if these tea mixtures did not help, then I was ready to die.

December approached. My daughter was planning to visit us from Italy. I asked my son-in-law to come with her, never mentioning why I asked them to come together. I was hiding the truth from them, believing that it would be much easier when they found out upon their arrival. They arrived one week before Christmas. Then I told them that I was seeing them for the last time, and I wanted to say goodbye before dying. They were dumbfounded. Antonio, my son-in-law, was very angry with me. He couldn't believe that I had kept this from them for such a long time, or that I had wasted so much precious time which I could have used for treatment.

He insisted that I should accept surgery. His uncle had the same problem, he explained, and after surgery he lived a normal life again. I took it into consideration. What should I do? My wife joined them. She could hardly wait for somebody to put pressure upon me. I consented to it, but not because I believed it would help, but to make my family happy. I called my urologist's office for an appointment.

Before entering the hospital, I was faced with the loss of my job. I asked for an appointment with my director, Dr. David Balsillie. I told him about my problem. Without blaming anybody, I explained my situation, and asked for a transfer to another group. I reminded him that since I had joined this group, problems were non-existent as well as, no down time at all. He verified this by checking his diary, and promised to do something for me. On the spot, with another supervisor, he arranged for my transfer.

On Friday, January the 6th, Dr. Balsillie called me back to his office. He explained my benefits to me. I knew I had six days full salary, and after that I would receive 67% of my wages. But I was concerned about what would happen to my seniority status. He explained that my seniority status was continuing in the same way as that for a permanent position. He used my overtime and my vacation to get me a seven-month full wage guaranty. He promised that after my hospital stay, I would start a new job with other people. But, as was soon evident it was too late. On Monday I entered the hospital and never went back to work again.

I don't know if I believed in my healing then, but deep down inside, a strong feeling was pouring out, and hope was building inside me that I would be cured, if only I could gain time. I felt a relief as though a big load had been lifted off my shoulders. My job would be saved, and I could concentrate on my healing. The fear of losing everything vanished suddenly. Again I saw a bright future ahead. Brighter than I could see just a few days ago. The pressure on my chest disappeared forever. For the first time in a long while, I smiled, and felt happy. "My job would be saved," I had an urge to cry out loudly. I wanted to bend over the desk and embrace that noble man. I was happy. I was infinitely happy. The few things that I had salvaged through the bankruptcy would be saved, and life would continue peacefully, as it had before. The cause of my disease was removed, and that was the first positive step in my war against cancer. Unfortunately, that wasn't enough.

I panicked, and at the same time felt of guilty conscience. Only now I realized how selfish I was, and thought only about myself. Yes, it was hard on me. Yes, I had suffered so much through my life. I was fed up with everything, and thought, the sooner I would be gone, the better off everybody will be. There was no cure for me anyway. In my selfishness I never thought about my family. How would they take it? In my narrow-mindedness I believed that it would be better for them too. When my suffering finished, their suffering would disappear too. Then doubt entered in. I asked myself, in great despair, when there is no hope, there is always the unanswered question in our mind "did we do everything we could?" In my selfishness I left them with that dilemma, for which they could have guilt feelings for the rest of their lives. I was afraid that everything was too late now, and I wanted to undergo the surgery right away.

I was to be admitted to the Hospital on January the 11th, 1984. I begged my urologist's secretary to move the date up. She explained that it was impossible, because the doctor was on vacation and was returning on January 9th. I had no choice. I had to wait.

Very modestly we celebrated Christmas Day. It was my saddest Christmas ever. I have had many difficult Christmas Days, but they were no comparison to this one. We never talked about my situation. We did everything not to ruin our Christmas spirit, knowing perhaps it was our last Christmas Day together. Deceptive hope was all we had. It was our last straw and we held on to it. I suffered the most, but I was also the bravest one. I tried not to think about it and kept my spirit high, hoping that everything was going to be all okay. My battle was not yet lost, and that was my consolation.

On January the 17th 1984 I underwent surgery. I was put under anaesthesia at 8:00 AM, and woke up late in the afternoon. It seemed as though it was evening because I awoke in a semi-dark room. It was my son-in-law's birthday. Nice birthday! ? He had to go back to Italy to take care of business. My daughter stayed on with her mother to be with her through this difficult time.

Upon awakening, I first saw my daughter. Behind her was my wife. They were only allowed to be with me for a short time in the intensive care unit. The condition that I was in speaks for itself, yet I was so happy to see my daughter at my bedside. It is needless to say how much I love her. Every parent loves his or her child, but she meant much, much more to me.

At a very early age I lost my mother. I was so young that I don't remember her face. Most of my sufferings were because I had lost her so early. My father remarried and brought a devil into the house. When I married, I prayed to God to give me a baby girl, so I could give her my mother's name and to shower her with love that I had never experienced. I know that my mother loved me very much, as she loved her other children, but moreso because I was her only son. But I couldn't remember that. The tomb that had closed on her, seemed to have put her love for me in the dark as well, and all my life I felt an enormous emptiness in my heart.

Therefore, when I say that my daughter is the most precious thing in the world to me, it is not only the love of a father for his child, but through her name, it is the love towards a parent as well. I was so happy to see her at my bedside. In my agony, I believed that this was the end. To die in her hands would be the sweetest death. Knowing how much I loved her and what she meant to me, my wife let her step forward to hold my hand during my awakening. My mind cleared a little, and I heard her calling: "Tata! Tata! Tata! ..." (Daddy! Daddy! Daddy!) I tried to smile and say something, but when I took a breath, the pain was so severe that I cried, choking, convulsed in a death rattle. The nurse came and put an oxygen mask on my face. I felt the oxygen streaming down to my lungs and I regained consciousness.

Dear God, what a feeling. My child, and her encouraging smile, gave me the will to fight, and it was a guarantee that I would win this battle and get well again. The anaesthesia made me delirious. Had it not been for the pain, which kept me on Earth, I would have felt as though I was already in Heaven, and there stood before me an Angel with my daughter's form. But the excruciating pain was a guarantee that there was no end to my sufferings. All my intestines cried in burning pain. If I could only breathe. If I could only move. Even a hand movement caused me excruciating pain, so I laid still.

As a young man I spent sometime in refugee camps, after which I sailed on merchant ships which, by all rights, I called pirates of the atomic age. These were Shipping Companies that had fled Yugoslavia after World War II. Most of them, like the one I was working for, stationed in the USA, and their ships sailed under Liberian or Panamanian flags. These were ships where seamen had no rights. They were treated like cargo. In the event of sickness, the company would disembark a seaman and send him to the country from where they took him, which in my case was Italy, holding no responsibility for him, despite whether he was crippled, dead or alive. I experienced this when I got tuberculosis, and the Company gave up on me too. Sailing on these ships, I travelled all around the world. I had seen many countries and customs. Returning to the refugee camp where my family had arrived, my wife asked me:

"Where are we planning to immigrate to?"

"There is one country where I would like to go," I said, "and if we can't go there, we are going back home, despite the consequences that are awaiting me as a political refugee."

That country was Canada, which I fell in love with, through Vancouver, where I had been five times as a sailor. Of this choice I was certain. I had known it all the time, but never so much as that night when I was in the intensive care unit. The nurse on duty never stopped for even a second to take a breath, and kept thinking of what to do next. She was always around me reading my temperature, my blood pressure, giving needles, adjusting pillows, wiping the sweat from my forehead, or just putting her hand on my forehead, which made me feel better, more secure and relaxed. This strange lady in white, looked after me as though I was a member of her family. I felt so secure. Then another nurse would come and replaced the first, equally as well as the previous. I know that there are many very reputable hospitals around the world, but considering the care given to me and to other patients that I had seen, I strongly believe that Canada is the best country in the world.

Two days after surgery I was transferred to the Bell Wing, to Room 664. There was another patient, who had the same kind of surgery as I, and his name was also Joe. My urologist visited me several times daily, the same as he did when I was in the intensive care unit. He explained to me that he had kept me on the operating table one and a half hours longer than expected because, he had much more to do than just remove my bladder.

In the Kosevo Hospital, Sarajevo, 1951, my decomposing right kidney was removed. My surgeon, Dr. Kovacevic didn't believe I would survive that surgery and consequently didn't clean the area out properly. At least twice a year I had an inflammation in that area. The pain would radiate down into my right leg. According to my urologist, not even the catheter was removed as medically required. It was left hanging in the spot where the kidney was. At the time that my bladder was removed, my whole right side was inflamed.

Josip Gabre

From July 1983 to January 1984 I had been in the Bell wing several times; therefore, I knew the hospital staff very well. I was very close to some of them. They even refered to me as a model patient. I had been ill so often in my life, with all kinds of sicknesses yet this was the worst so far. Yet throughout it all I never changed. I patiently suffered and tried to take care of myself, in order not to be a bother to the people trying to take care of me.

I have to compliment the Bell wing staff, whom I considered the best of friends. Being diabetic, it was very hard to keep my blood sugar down. The endocrinologists did miracles in my case. My sugar was under control and the wound was healing quickly.

During the operation, six inches of the descending colon was cut. A catheter was connected to it to drain the urine to a plastic pouch, which is connected to the right side of my abdomen. No bowel could go through the connected part of the intestine, so I was fed intravenously, and for several days I had a plastic tube connected through my nose to my stomach for drainage. Since I was recovering very quickly, the tube was removed, and I started to eat; first liquid food, and then solid. I was already walking around. I ate the food, but I had no bowel movements. Before long I had severe pain in my stomach, which got worse every day.

Even a "professional" patient, as I considered myself, can be wrong. I strongly believed that the pain in the stomach was postsurgical and that it would disappear. When the pain intensified I called the nurse and told her about it. Led by experience, she quickly called the doctor on duty. He came at once, and checked if my stomach and intestines were working properly. Nothing. My stomach and intestines were dead silent. Nothing was happening there. He gave me some medication. A few minutes later,

I vomited, undigested food (everything that I had eaten in the last few days). All doctors from the ward rushed to my bedside. They listened for signs from my intestines. Nothing. The head doctor then ordered the reinstallation of drainage back in my stomach again.

I was so disappointed and unhappy. I knew that there were complications. I could see it in the doctors' faces. I could see it in all the attention given to me. The drainage wasn't ready until that evening. When the doctor on duty arrived to install it, I told him that my stomach and intestines were working again. He listened, and sure enough they were.

Overhearing the doctor's conversation, I understood that emergency surgery was considered to find out what had happened with my stomach and intestines. They believed that the complications were caused by rapidly spreading cancer.

The young resident doctor, who was to install the drainage again, decided not to do so. His senior colleague was angry with him, but when he listened himself, he was satisfied with the decision and agreed with his younger colleague. I was so relieved because the installation of that plastic tube would have been too much for me. Three days later I was dismissed from the hospital, as everything seemed to be all right.

S. G. worked in the health food store (For Your Health) across the street from me. She had graduated from reflexology and was keen on health food products. When my wife told her that I was in the hospital, she came to visit me. She didn't feel she could offer any help to me then, but when I came home, she visited me twice a week and gave me reflexology treatment. She suggested that I should go on a vegetarian diet, and recommended freshly made vegetable juices. Immediately I accepted the advice. Others cured themselves with a macrobiotic diet alone, so what had I to lose? In lieu of macrobiotic food, a vegetarian diet would do just as well, I thought. Reading many books, I found out how good a vegetarian diet is for our body. This would be the first step in cleansing my system and restoring my immune system too. I thought too, that it could stop cancer from spreading around. Please, note that this was not a 'total' vegetarian diet that I went on. As I was unable to find macrobiotic food, I went on the diet which as a small boy I grew up on, before World War II. I stopped eating meat, and I had fish several times a week.

I bought a centrifugal juicemaker, and drank fresh vegetable juice on an empty stomach, every morning. I had to find a protein substitute, so I started sprouting. Beans (legumes), during sprouting, release great amounts of proteins, vitamins and minerals. My urologist recommended that I eat food containing fibre. As a rule, my diet then consisted of one daily meal of brown rice or barley, mixed with vegetables and different kinds of beans. My stool had always been a problem but nothing compared to what I experienced then. Because of my new diet, my stool improved.

Approximately a month and a half after surgery, I felt a strange pain in my lower back. I had never experienced this kind of pain before. A dull pain would start around four o'clock in the afternoon, and would last until four o'clock in the morning. The cycle repeated itself precisely to the minute. During that time, I couldn't sit, lie down, or walk; absolutely nothing. One doesn't scream from this kind of pain, but if I could only find its source! Massaging the suspected area, I felt no relief. At this time my stool worsened. I was constipated for over two weeks. My family doctor gave me several different kinds of laxatives to take one by one, and recommended I stay with the one that worked best. I did so, but none of them worked. I then took all of them at once. Again, nothing happened. I then took two enemas. I cleansed myself, but I bled through the penis. I had an appointment with my urologist within a couple of days, but having seen the blood, I called him and told him what had happened. He ordered me to come to the hospital immediately. From his concerned voice, I knew that there was something very wrong. When I arrived at his office he took me in and examined me.

After a short examination he said. "That damn thing has spread to your rectum".

I was again admitted to the Hospital. I again shared a room with a man, who, in great agony, was dying from cancer. It was horrible to watch him. Choking in a death rattle, he waved his hands, catching something unseen in the air, and only moments later pushing that something away. An indescribable fear appeared in his wide-open eyes. Did he see something in his hallucinations, I wondered? For hours and hours I watched him, and through his agony, I tried to penetrate into the secrets of death. I was afraid that I would soon experience the same agony.

As I have stated before, I have been sick often, and each time I cured myself with food. When I had no appetite, I forced myself to eat, to preserve my body's strength, helping it to fight disease. But this time I lost my appetite. I couldn't bear the sight of food, especially hospital food. My wife brought me a bowl of vegetable soup and some apples every evening, and I forced myself to eat all of it. I knew, to gain strength, I had to eat. Also, I was aware that cancer was spreading, and nothing could stop it anymore.

Within two days I was transferred to a private room, where I had all the time to think. All kinds of tests were done on me. The Cat-scan showed that cancer had now spread to my liver.

A friend of mine, Fulvio Baici, was with me when my urologist came to tell me about the analysis.

"Joe," the doctor said, "that damn thing has spread to your liver."

"Is that possible?" I asked calmly, without any commotion.

"Yes, the instruments showed it, and there is no doubt."

"Well," I said, still very calmly, "there is nothing that I can do about it. Can I? If instruments showed it, then it must be the truth."

He promised to send liver specialists to see me. When the doctor left, and the two of us remained alone, Fulvio asked in awe:

"Joe, I don't understand, how can you be so cool? I was looking at you when the doctor told you the horrible news. You didn't blush. You didn't blink. Your voice didn't fail you. Nothing. If somebody had offered me a cup of coffee, I would have reacted more."

"Fulvio," I said, fighting back the tears, "it is not easy. You know what it means. It is all finished. I can do nothing about it, and I have made up my mind, because there is no hope anymore. I have to get ready for a long, long journey, and I am ready to go. Inevitably everybody has to go anyway."

As soon as Fulvio left, I phoned my wife to tell her the bad news. She wailed loudly, as though somebody had stabbed her. I felt the pain in my throat, and for the first time I regretted being honest. On my side of the telephone line I felt all her agony. I felt my heart break and asked myself: why did I tell her that news? Why didn't I conceal it from her and let it develop slowly, so she could, in time, prepare herself for the worst?

She phoned our family physician who was a good friend too. He tried to console her as best he could, and promised to see her that evening. Many other patients came to console me when they heard the bad news. One of them, William Carswell, stood by me for a long time, trying to brighten my spirits in addition to trying hard to keep my mind off the dreadful news. At that moment I wanted to remain alone, and I told him so. He left with the promise that he wouldn't be away for long.

So, the time of truth had arrived. Without any doubt, this is the period when everybody panics over the unknown: the patient, his family, friends, relatives and even his physician, especially when he has become a friend, as my doctor had. This time everybody panicked, everybody except me. I was perfectly calm. I had endured enough suffering for now, and had no intention of suffering any longer. When I was left alone, I closed my eyes and began to think. I tried to recall events from the past; both good and bad ones. The bad ones prevailed, and I dwelled on them with strange peacefulness. Was it cowardice, or was it knowledge that everything was lost, and that there was no hope left? Is it the feeling that overcomes everybody who is terminally ill? Was this the feeling that engulfs every human who is condemned to death, and has to think about it all the time? I thought of my wife and my daughter. I knew how much they would miss me.

Moved by all these feelings, I cried. Why? I knew that everybody had to go inevitably. There was no mystery about that, yet no matter how much we try, we are never prepared for death. I tried to imagine what would happen when that moment arrived. Is this the end to everything we know, or is it the beginning of something else? I had read much on reincarnation and I strongly believed that this was not the end. Even at the time when I was an atheist, I believed that there was something else beyond this life.

Josip Gabre

What? How? I couldn't say, but I strongly believed that this was not the end. This realization filled me with peacefulness, and a strange sort of happiness. I contemplated on the meaning of life and on existence of humanity. Was it possible that a perfect being such as man came from nothing and vanishes into nothingness?

Deliberating so, I considered the human brain. According to scientific research, only 3% of the human brain is put to use and even the greatest minds (Einstein) use only 7% of its capacity. Is it possible that all this is simply destroyed? Does the Creator, God or nature, whichever your preference, waste the human mind; such perfection, which created miracles on this planet? Not so long ago I stopped believing that what is here on the earth is unique and that what comes after is nothing. Several times I had seen the movie "Beyond and Back", and met people who had such an experience. Did they lie to me? Was all that was happening around me, just an illusion; religion, nature, consciousness, ideals, God, everything we can think of, see and touch with our hands? A strange peace overwhelmed me and I wept silently.

I wept without pain, without remorse, without fear. What would happen when everything, around me, disappeared? I couldn't believe that I would be separated from my family, my relatives and my friends.

When I had fled my homeland and was separated from my family, I had felt more depressed than I did now. Then I had no faith. I sailed across the Adriatic sea in a small rowboat, at the worst time of the year, when the sea was full of surprises. Then I strongly believed I was seeing them for the last time, and my heart was tearing apart. Now, I strongly believed that the separation would be a very short one, and that we would meet again in another dimension in another form. How, where and what, I didn't know, but I strongly believed it would be so. If only this suffering would come to an end; both mine and my family's. I always hated abrupt changes, and this was a very abrupt one.

Mixed emotions overwhelmed me; peace and trepidation at the same time. If we had come to this world with a task to fulfil, had I fulfilled mine, I asked. If I hadn't, would I come back to this planet again? There was no way that I wanted to come back again. Once departed from this world, I never wished to come back, despite the possibilities. My experiences in this world disgusted me so much, that departure from it seemed like a relief. I don't know if everybody asks so many questions in the last moments of their lives and picks through the past to justify or judge their deeds, but I did.

Very early in my life I was taught how to appreciate and practice the best human values. I absorbed those teachings, like a man in a desert who would drink his last drop of water and remain thirsty. I lived that way all my life. When I was hungry, and my life, as everybody elses around me, depended on two very small pieces of bread daily, I gave it to somebody weaker than I. Even when those who taught me these values, failed, and abandoned these teachings, I never changed, because I believed that in doing good to others, indirectly, I helped myself. In the same way, by doing harm to others, I would harm myself. Is this the reason we came into this world? If it was, then I had fulfilled my task. Looking back, I had nothing to be ashamed of. I had no reason to fear death.

Mr. McLean, the terminally ill cancer patient, was transferred to a single room. I can't explain it, but every time in passing his room, I stopped to visit him. Sometimes I would stay with him for a long time. Why? I don't know, but there must have been a reason for which I had no explanation. Maybe I hoped to uncover something, which was up to that time unknown to me. Maybe I was expecting to unveil the mystery of death, and to find the insight of a peaceful departure. As usual, he wasn't aware of anything around him. As always, he was swinging his hands as though grabbing something invisible while choking insufferably with fear on his face. Does he see something, I asked myself repeatedly? Afterwards, I would go back to my room, lie down on my bed and think. Life around me was slowing and in the calmness of my soul I listened to it, as though some very distant and unattainable humming.

That same afternoon I was visited by three liver specialists. They did further tests on me. The first things they looked at, were my eyes, to see if there were any changes. They shook their heads in disbelief, and told me openly that it was quite unlikely that cancer had spread to my liver. They arranged to have thorough tests done with the most sensitive instruments at the Hospital.

My wife came to visit me in the evening, as she did every day. She was weeping, and I couldn't console her.
"You will see," I said to her, "everything is going to be OK, don't worry."
"How is it going to be OK?" she said, through sobs. "Your cancer has spread to your liver. Do you know what that means?"
"I know," I said very calmly, "but trust me just a little. You will see, everything is going to be alright."

I never told her what I meant. If I died, everything would be alright, because she wouldn't suffer any longer watching my suffering. With time she would adjust to life without me, and in her mind would remain just memories, both the painful ones of course, and also pleasant memories of me that noone could take away from her. If I got well, which at that time I didn't believe, we would continue to live as we did before and everything would be just fine. I decided that I would never give her bad news again. I wanted to spare her from any further suffering, to hide everything, and endure the pain without showing the slightest sign of how much I suffered. When the time came, she would slowly adjust to it. I made her rush home where our family doctor waited for her. What could he tell her that she didn't already know? As our physician and dear friend, he would at least console her.

The next day I was to be examined by the most sensitive instruments the Hospital had. The results were sent to my urologist the same day. The analysis showed that my liver was still clean. It was a relief for everybody. I had to tell my wife the good news as soon as possible. She phoned our daughter in Italy, who wanted to come back to Canada. My daughter phoned me from Italy, and insisted on coming over. I didn't want my situation to put a strain on her life. I promised her that if it was necessary, I would call her.

My urologist, upon bringing me the good news wanted to talk to me. We had to make a decision about what to do next.
"You don't want to have another pouch?" he asked.
"No, no way", I said firmly.
"There are only two things left", he said, "radiation or chemotherapy."
"Doctor," I said "no chemotherapy, even if I have to die here, this very moment."
"What do you say about radiation?"

I knew what radiation treatment was, more or less, but I wasn't sure if it could do me any damage. Therefore, I asked my urologist for a detailed explanation. The fact that radiation attacks only cancer and does not harm the rest of the human body, as he explained to me, convinced me to consent to it. I agreed to radiation mostly because I was convinced that radiation would not shorten my life, which, with chemotherapy was not so, and more than anything else I wanted to relieve my conscience. I knew however, that radiation treatment would not cure me.

Years later I realized how misinformed I was about radiation. Led by the desire to help others, I spoke about my experiences on the radio program "Sounds of Croatia" on CHIN Radio Station in Toronto, which I hosted in the absence of producer Mr. John Loncaric. Many people phoned me for information and advice. Late in 1988 Helga phoned. She told me she had intestinal cancer, and after every radiation treatment, she had to have surgery to remove part of her intestine, which was completely dry, due to the radiation treatment. My physician had never told me this. I refused to have another plastic pouch, but having agreed to have radiation treatment, another plastic pouch was inevitable. If this were to happen, I would be dead now.

Just before my release from the Hospital, Interferon treatment was considered. It was a new medicine and little was known about it. A student nurse brought me all available literature about Interferon, to prepare me for eventual side effects. I paid little attention to the articles because I knew that I was dying. Later, during my recovery, I found out more about Interferon. It is a protein, a product of our body, which fights infections. Earlier research with Interferon suggested that it could be successful against breast, bone and lymphatic cancer. Perhaps it was my luck that they had none of it available at the Hospital. Now, in this new condition, with cancer in my rectum and spreading further, Interferon could not be considered.

The damage had already been done. At that point there was little possibility that anything could help me, despite what it was. I just wanted to clear my conscience. The next day I was taken to the Princess Margaret Hospital. I was in excruciating pain and it got worse each day. Unable to walk, I was put in a wheel chair. With the Lanark simulator, the position of cancer was found. The next day I came back for radiation treatment.

Before the treatment, several nurses or doctors, I don't know which for sure, examined me. Then my oncologist arrived. She explained what she would be doing, what radiation treatment is, and what the effect would be.

"Doctor," I asked, "how long do I have to live?"

She looked at me.

"Do you really want to know?" she asked.

"Yes," I repeated. "I have a very important job to do before I go from this world, and I would like to know how much time I have left to finish it."

"Joe," she said. "We can't cure you. I hope you understand that. With my own knowledge, optimistically speaking, you have one year."

"Thank you doctor," I said "that is enough."

She looked at me for some time, as though she wanted to correct herself, and she said:

"For some patients I have given only three months, and they live for three, four and more years. There were those I gave three years, and they died after four months. You never know what is going to happen from one day to the next."

"If I am correct, you don't expect that I could die suddenly, say within a couple of months?"

She smiled at me, and gave no answer.

Earlier in my life I had an experience about which I couldn't speak openly. Now the time of truth had arrived, and I had a guilty conscience. I went through the worst prisoner camp in human history. Now dying, I was taking that secret with me. Due to the situation at that time, I was afraid, for one reason or another, that nobody would be able to talk about it.

Before me, many had gone, unfortunate and innocent, as I was. Who knows how many are still alive, waiting for rehabilitation that will never come? With excruciating pain, I started to write down my memoirs, to leave behind a testimony for some future historian, who would write about it. While I was in severe pain I couldn't write. I couldn't think, or walk or do anything. Painkillers alleviated the pain. While under sedation, I vegetated, motionless, unable to think, to concentrate or do anything. When the effects of the painkillers subsided and just before the pain became unbearable, I would get down to work. That was for a very short period of time, and I would sit behind the typewriter pounding with my fingers with such frenzy, continuing until I could no longer endure the pain. (From that manuscript I published the non fiction novel by the title: "THE SEED FROM THE STONE).

I went to St. Mary's drugstore on Yonge Street, to purchase some vitamins and painkillers. Everybody knew me in that drugstore, because I was there so often. Vickers Head, who worked there, approached me. He knew my case, as everybody did. He excused himself, only to reappear after a few moments. In his hands he had several sheets of paper, legal size, typed on both sides.

"Read this," he said, "maybe this will help you."

CHAPTER SIX

PAU D'ARCO (TAHEEBO)

Spring, 1982 Issue
Herb for all reasons

(Tabebuia altissima)
"What is new is not necesarily true,
what is true is not necesarily new"

By Louise Tenney

South American physicians are using the inner bark of two South American trees to successfully treat various forms of cancer, including leukemia, and other debilitating diseases. A tea is made with the inner bark of *Lapacho Colorado* or *Lapacho Morado (Tabebuia Avellanedae* or *Tabebuia Altisima)*. These trees are commonly known as *Ipe roxo* or *Pau D'Arco*. The Indian name for them is *Taheebo*. They are tall ozoniferous trees with extremely deep roots that grow in places abundant with ozone. Ozone air is fresh and pure in that, it is free of pollutants such as smog, exhaust, smoke and pesticides. These two species have beautiful flowers, one purple and one red, which are carnivorous in that they eat insects. Scientific research has found substances in the bark that produce uncommon resistance to fungus and spores, although nearby vegetation is covered with it.

Taheebo was originally used by the South American Indians called Callawaya, **descendants of the Inca** medicine men, to cure cancer and many other debilitating diseases and was rediscovered about 20 years ago by two Brazilian physicians, Drs. T. Meyer, and P. Ruiz, who have been treating and using this herb with fantastic results. Brazilian newspapers and magazines devote whole pages to the marvellous cures attributed to Taheebo (Pau D'Arco). Today, Taheebo is widely used in hospitals and clinics in Brazil and is available to the public in pharmacies and herbal shops. Many doctors recommend it as a therapeutic herbal tea. Under the direction of Dr. Meyer, Taheebo has been distributed to cancer patients throughout Argentina and to doctors throughout South America. According to him, Taheebo heals wounds, combats infection, stimulates the appetite, and acts as a general, all-round tonic.

Based on their experience, both American and South American physicians have concluded that the tea somehow **stimulates and apparently strengthens the immune system.** Through an analysis of extract samples of the herb, the Dietmann Research Foundation of Los Angeles found that it acts as a stimulant to the alimentary tract through the rectum and then back to the liver, gall bladder and sweat glands. The sweat glands serve the important bodily function of relief valves for the stomach, lungs and heart. The stimulating effect Taheebo has on the body can be explained in two ways. First, it helps keep the sweat glands open and operating, thus helping the elimination of stomach, heart and lung problems. Second, it warns the body when the adrenal glands are under stress.

Taheebo has been most successful in cases considered hopeless by traditional medicine. It has been said to give greater vitality to the body by strengthening its organic defenses, revitalizing the body, helping to create new and normal cells, increasing resistance to diseases, creating a feeling of well-being and helping to alleviate **pain**. Unlike prescription drugs, it can be taken in large quantities and in **combination with any other medication without the risk of harmful effects.** It can be used by children and adults alike. According to Dr. Meyer's experience, a gradual elimination of pain is evident after only a few days of treatment.

Mr. Millie, who has brought Taheebo to Canada, explains that Taheebo actually **breaks down the protective casing around the cancer tumour** that prevents a normal supply of oxygen and nourishment from the blood stream.

The herb contains a high percentage of easily assimilated iron. Drs. Meyer and Ruiz studied the chemical composition and found it to contain powerful antibiotic properties, and substances effective in eliminating pain. The antibiotic properties seem to combat **nefarious germs** that **cause nearly all diseases.**

Reports from the U. S. A. and South America suggest that Taheebo has contributed immensely to the elimination and/or alleviation of some symptoms associated with the following dysfunctions:

ACTS AS BLOOD BUILDER
ACTS AS A TONIC
ALLERGIES
ANEMIA
ARTERIOSCLEROSIS
ASTHMA
BRONCHITIS
CANCER (all types)
COLITIS

DEPRESSION, INSOMNIA & ANXIETY
DIABETES
ECZEMA
GASTRITIS
GONORRHEA
HEMORRHOIDS
INFECTIONS
LEUKEMIA
LUPUS
PARKINSON'S DISEASE
PSORIASIS AND SKIN DISEASE
PYORRHOEA
RELIEVES PAIN
RHEUMATISM
RINGWORM
SPLEEN INFECTIONS
ULCERS
VARICOSE VEINS
WOUNDS (heals)

Taheebo is most widely used by **cancer** patients and **allergy** sufferers. Interviews with allergists confirm the herb works, although not for everyone. A matter of weeks may be all it takes for some remissions, but months are more often required. However, the patient may have to change other factors affecting his condition before the benefit of this tea can be realized. But remissions have been seen that are permanent (for most kinds of cancer, this will be 5 years from initial disappearance of the disease).

Since this herb helps in ridding the system of toxic substances, the body is given new vitality, which in turn affects spirit and mind. The agony of depression, **insomnia** and pathological **anxiety** has often been greatly relieved by Taheebo.

It has been suggested as a potential prophylactic if not therapeutic for AIDS (acquired immune deficiency syndrome). And there are reports of excellent results in patients with Herpes simplex, and diverse other perplexing skin conditions.

ACTUAL CASE HISTORIES:

CANCER

Dr. Orlando dei Santi from Brazil heard about Taheebo, took the bark, boiled it in white wine, mixed the still hot brew with orange juice, and took it to the Santo Andre Municipal Hospital where his brother was dying of cancer. He noticed that the pain immediately disappeared and he could sleep soundly. After taking Taheebo for a month, he was discharged from the hospital. A thorough examination showed that he had no trace of cancer remaining.

A Utah woman, who had been suffering from cancer for over a year, started to drink Taheebo tea and experienced a relief from pain within 24 hours. She continued to drink the tea on a daily basis and after several weeks, remained free from her initial pain.

A woman living in South America experienced such unbearable pain from cancer of the womb that she was prepared to take her own life to end her suffering. After taking the tea for ten days, the constant pain and bleeding stopped and she recovered admirably after that.

A Florida man, diagnosed as suffering from prostate cancer, used the Taheebo herb for several months. After the first 13 days he experienced an unusual feeling of well-being. **By elimi-**

nating white sugar products and by supplementing his diet with natural vitamins and minerals, he noticed a marked increase in the effect of the herb. When I spoke with him in March 1982, he told me that he was informed by his doctors that his cancer was now completely gone.

A woman from Oregon claims that the malignant tumours in her bladder disappeared after using this herb. She said it was confirmed by her physician at Kaiser Hospital.

Another man attributes this herb to healing the cancer on his face, and, his arthritis.

PYORRHOEA

An Illinois man who was suffering from pyorrhoea, a painful disease of the gums that usually develops into an abscess, found himself making regular trips to the dentist. The dentist's treatment consisted of lancing and draining the abscess and prescribing antibiotics. Pyorrhoea caused this man a great deal of anxiety because as the disease progresses, the results are manifested in a gradual loosening of the teeth that ultimately leads to extraction of the teeth. This man began taking Taheebo in November, 1981, and after using it for 24 hours, he noticed some extremely remarkable results. It resulted in a subsiding of the pain, a diminishment in the swelling of the gums and an elimination of the pus pockets embedded in the gums; this enabled him to retain his teeth.

DIABETES

I talked to another woman in Oregon who has a friend with diabetes and kidney failure, and has almost died three times. The doctors were really concerned because his whole body chemistry was way off balance. After taking a cup of Taheebo tea daily, for ten days, his body chemistry was normal. The doctors couldn't believe his turnabout, for they hadn't expected him to live for very long.

REJUVENATION

Dr. Paul Stein of LaJolla, California writes: "...As I continued to take TAHEEBO for a few days, I had the feeling of being generally but slowly and deeply rejuvenated. My endurance, mind, sense of smell, strength, tolerance of cold, and general well-being was tremendously improved. My work productivity is about ten times what it was before October 17 (1981). These effects are continuing and are increasing."

DOCTORS' TESTIMONIALS

Professor Walter Accorsi stated: "From my first experiments with it, I learned two important things that greatly encouraged me concerning cancer. First, red PAU D'ARCO **eliminates the pains caused by the disease;** and secondly, it **multiplies the amount of red corpuscles.** Our amazement grew. This bark helps everything. Ulcers, diabetes and rheumatism - the TAHEEBO tea helped them all. What impressed us most was the time it took to achieve the results: Usually less than one month! A childhood friend, Col. Amatea, residing in the city of Itu, had an ailing wife. She was on the verge of death from intestinal cancer. She had been operated on five times in eight months, to little avail. After just one day of treatment with Taheebo, she slept peacefully for the first time in eight months. More than that, she was soon well. That was years ago and she has stayed well. Anyone who is skeptical should contact Col. Amatea."

Dr. Octaviano Gaiarsa stated: "Many of my colleagues speak of help for diabetes, of osteomyelitis and even cancer. I personally know of cases of help for anaemia, authenticated with count of corpuscles, and of various ulcers after 15 days, or at the most, one month of treatment. **I had a case of advanced leukemia - 240,000 leukocytes (white cells) per cubic mm of blood. After one month of treatment the number of white cells was down to 20,000, which is considered normal.** That case would otherwise have been fatal. The Taheebo tree itself has uncommon resistance. Any type of vegetation, when exposed to water and the weather, eventually gets covered with spores that lead to a formation of fungus. This does not occur to the Pau D'Arco (Taheebo)."

Physicians at the Municipal Hospital in Santo Andre have noticed that the pain suffered by patients with leukemia or other cancer **disappeared within hours** after they received the brew made from Taheebo. They also found that **within 30 days of treatment,** most patients no longer showed any symptoms of the dreaded disease. They also noticed that many other afflictions, such as diabetes, would disappear even more quickly than the cancer.

This may indeed sound incredible, but it only confirms the work that is being done in South America by **Doctors Teodoro Meyer and Prats Ruiz.** They have been working with this herb for years and have reported excellent results with terminally sick patients.

The results were so amazing that these cures spurred further research. The University of Illinois confirms the research in Brazil, and the claims that Taheebo does indeed contain a substance that is highly effective against cancers. While many herbs are credited with properties that stop cancer cell growth, it is said that Taheebo contains a compound called **quechua,** a powerful antibiotic with virus-killing properties. These properties were found by Dr. Meyer to eliminate pain almost immediately and multiply the amount of **red corpuscles.**

CHAPTER SEVEN

(THE FOUR T's IN ATTITUDE)

This is the remedy for me, I concurred. The fact that **Taheebo** or **Pau D'Arco**, whichever you prefer, rejuvenates good, healthy cells and helps the body to fight disease, was for me extraordinary, and it was what I had been searching for. My stubborn belief that I would get well only if I found something that would help my body to fight disease, materialized. Immediately I bought some capsules with pulverized Taheebo and some for brewing tea. Vickers explained how to prepare it, and when I came home I started to take it, between fifteen and twenty capsules that first day, and one gallon of tea. I thought, if the dosage was not restricted, then the more I take of it, the more it would help me. I could not compromise. I knew if I didn't kill cancer as soon as possible, it would kill me, and I played my last card.

The next day, S. G., my reflexologist, came to see me. That day, for the first time, I felt some warmth going from my feet up my legs, and it felt so good. I suddenly realized that I hadn't taken any painkillers that morning, and that I had slept well the night before. I had been taking painkillers only in extreme necessity. I also remembered having had breakfast, and that for the first time since I had been ill, eaten with a hearty appetite. I had awakened feeling hungry and ate everything prepared for me.

"Suzy," I said. "Something is happening. I feel much better this morning, better than I have felt in a long time, and that goes far, far back, before my illness."

She wanted to know everything in detail, and I gave her my observations of the past twenty four hours. I gave her the article by Louise Tenney, so that she too, could see if there were any similarities with my case. We agreed that my experience was the same as those described in that report. I had thirteen more radiation therapy sessions to take, one each week. During that time a blood test was taken regularly, and it was always normal. It never got worse during the therapy. That was a very good sign, because I had heard of others who had trouble with that, and were then treated for it. I was supposed to experience problems and setbacks during radiation of the descending colon (rectum), which I had never been told about. This didn't happen either. Why? Then, I had no answer.

Fifteen therapy sessions were concluded. I felt very good. I was not constipated and felt no pain nor any other discomfort. I used this time to finish my manuscript. Up to now, it had been very difficult to do so because of the pain. I was afraid that the situation could get worse. What I had learned about cancer up to that point, made me aware that it can reappear anytime, and I couldn't allow it to take me by surprise. I kept myself very busy and did everything possible to use this time wisely, to finish the many things I had planned long ago, and had been putting aside for one reason or another.

At this point I would like to focus on attitude. I would like to compare my attitude to that of another individual. A friend of mine was in another Hospital with a malignant tumour. Maybe the difference between the two of us was that I had been ill all my life, and he had never been ill until that time. For him, to get sick for the first time and with such an incurable disease, was of great psychological magnitude. I strongly believe that he gave up too soon. I begged him to join with me and fight the cancer together. He never took my advice. He listened to nobody. Instead of taking all possible steps to cleanse himself from the toxins deposited in his body, he poisoned himself even more. He ate improperly and instead of quitting smoking, he smoked more than before.

What is one cigarette more or less, or one hot dog more or less for a dying man? In those last moments everything seems hopeless. Is our mind pushing us to extremes during our last days? Must we relish all the pleasures of life irrationally in the little time left? What do these earthly pleasures mean when time is limited? I personally believe that under these circumstances we mustn't fool ourselves. We must face our condition as it presents itself, realistically and without illusions. We can't make plans anymore, because we cannot fulfil them. We have to force ourselves to do everything possible that may help us.

We must ask ourselves, did we do everything in our power to bring back our health? If we didn't, then we owe this last effort to ourselves and to our families. If there is no hope, then we owe this effort to God (or the unknown). Is there anything after this life, and what is it? It is our last chance to look inside ourselves, and to cleanse our conscience in the face of the unknown. I know how hard last moments are, because I had met them. I wasn't afraid to die, maybe because I had a clear conscience. For a long time I experienced changes within myself, through which I slowly prepared myself for dying. I knew how much that friend of mine wanted to live. I knew how much he clung to even the smallest pleasures that life had offered him. "Yes", he used to say, " I will fight", but those words were empty, with no meaning to him or to anybody else.

I believe that one day science will have unquestionable proof of how attitude controls our well-being. Stress caused my illness but shouldn't I have been able to cope with it? We can preprogram ourselves in a healing direction too. I don't see why anybody should yield to a weakness, which could cause all our troubles, if behaviour in that direction is pushing us to the grave. With his behaviour, that friend of mine, made himself, and everybody else around him, miserable. I, on the contrary, didn't want anybody around me to suffer because of my own sufferings. I was always an optimist. Even when I had unbearable pain, I did everything to keep occupied to prevent thinking about my illness. As I said before, I started to write the book. When I couldn't write it, I switched off my mind and tried not to think about anything.

Reading about cancer, I came upon cases where people cured themselves with autosuggestion only. I did the same thing in my own way. My oncologist had given me only one year to live, yet I worked on this book as though I would live for a long time to come. Furthermore, I engaged in many hobbies. In doing so I gained doubly. First, I didn't think about my illness and secondly, I enriched myself with new experiences. I thought, if there was anything beyond this life, then everything that we gathered through our minds could be taken with us on that long journey with our soul. If there is reincarnation, and we come back to this planet, or we go to another sphere, then the experience from this world would be of some use to us. That is, of course, if the human mind is indestructible and follows the soul. If not, then we can be satisfied that we used our time wisely and enriched ourselves with a new experience, even when the going was rough.

Approximately fifteen days after the radiation treatments ended, I had an appointment with my Dr. urologist. He examined me.

"Hm, is this possible? Is this possible?" He repeated himself often. "This thing is shrinking," he said.

He asked his secretary to telephone my Dr. oncologist, at Princess Margaret Hospital. In my presence he told her about the news. She couldn't believe it, she said. I could make out what she was saying by my urologist's responses.

"I don't care if it is possible or not," he said, "but this is what I found with him."

He asked her if she had given me the maximum dosage of radiation, and if she could give me some more. The answer was negative and they agreed to give me another shot of radiation before my departure for Europe. Doctor urologist and doctor oncologist strongly believed that radiation had been responsible for my improvement, although they had used it as a last resort. They were aware of what usually happens to a patient when undergoing this kind of radiation treatment, yet they still believed radiation was beneficial to me. I disagreed with them and I had reason to do so. I knew why the change had come about, but I didn't want to mention it, knowing that I would open a can of worms, and get myself into a controversy that, then, I couldn't prove with other evidence. They would only deny the beneficial role of Taheebo tea in my case, and I would end up talking to a brick wall. So I continued taking Taheebo tea, I kept dieting, and I felt fantastic.

Doctor oncologist was right by saying that it was impossible to obtain such results with radiation treatment in a case such as mine, and doctor urologist couldn't contradict her. What was happening with me was new to them, and they had never read anything like this in medical textbooks. They knew nothing about Taheebo and its healing powers. Because of the radiation treatments, they had anticipated complications, damage, the drying out of, and the damage to my intestines. In my case, none of it happened. Since these predicted complications didn't come about, something else must have entered the picture to remedy my condition. They never asked if I had been taking or doing something on my own, although my urologist did have an idea because I had previously mentioned to him that I wouldn't rely on conventional medicine only. Taheebo! ? The word raced through my mind, and as much as I wanted to question it, I had no other answer. Taheebo, repeatedly, only Taheebo. Along with Taheebo I did practice a strict vegetarian diet, I meditated and I did many other things, including the radiation treatments. Radiation had helped nobody else, so how could I be so different? Diet, despite how beneficial it could be, couldn't bring me this kind of relief, and so quickly too. The change happened the very moment I started taking Taheebo tea, as I have described before. Repeatedly I had to go back to that fact. Taheebo brought a change in my situation. Taheebo was curing me.

A month before my departure to Europe, my urologist was surprised even more. During his examination he found that the tumour had shrunk so much that he was astounded, and very pleased also. He looked at me with a smile.

"You know something," he said "we aren't going to give you any more radiation treatments. I know you are taking something. I don't know what it is, and I don't want to know, but, by God, it is helping you. Continue with it, go to Europe, and when you come back, we will see what has happened."

So, unwillingly, my urologist admitted that something that I was taking, on my own, was helping me, and it was not medicine, or anything else that my physicians had given me. Therefore I have to repeat it again, Taheebo helped me and nothing else.

I felt great. Frankly, I had not felt so good in the last thirty years. The pain on the right side of my abdomen, caused by a badly performed operation in Sarajevo in 1951, disappeared completely. My stool movement was normal, and I checked its content regularly. There was no reason for doing so, but my condition had forced me into the habit of controlling everything. Then one day I noticed something mushroom like. At times these pieces were quite big. I strongly believe that if I had a microscope, I would have discovered that these mushroom like pieces were actually pieces of tumour.

LaDean Griffin, in her book HEALTH IN THE SPACE AGE, accentuates how the elimination of toxins, accumulated in our body, is important. Elimination, she says, happens in many different ways, through the urine, the sweat, the cough, but mostly through the stool. She warns us to be careful. If this process occurs too quickly, it can be dangerous to the organs through which elimination occurs. Our organs, such as our kidneys, can be overburdened and death can occur. When healing from cancer occurs, dead cancer cells have to be disposed of, in some way, and this is where rapid cleansing can become dangerous. Within cancer patients, the system cleanses itself constantly, since the body can fight cancer.

I have noticed that among cancer patients, including myself, when a crisis occurs, we tend to become constipated. No matter what kind of cancer one may have, and no matter where it may be located, constipation shows an adverse condition. The glands in our rectum absorb everything from the stool. This is then filtered and recycled through our liver. The longer we are constipated, the more toxins the liver has to filter. The liver weakens, and becomes highly infected. Talking to different people with descending colon or rectum cancer, I learned that after a long period of constipation, liver cancer occurred. This explains my urologist's concern about my liver. I had started to become terribly constipated when cancer had spread to my rectum. A good stool is of utmost importance for a healthy body.

By maintaining a partly vegetarian diet I managed to control my stool. Every evening before bedtime, I took one capsule of Cascara Sagrata, and a prune stew. Cascara Sagrata (Rhamnur purshiana) is an herbal laxative. It is more a regulator than a laxative, and it is derived from the pulverized bark of the cascara plant. In her report, Louise Tenney says that Taheebo also helps natural assimilation and elimination. I spoke to many people who had experienced intensified elimination upon taking Taheebo. Their fears were unfounded because Taheebo readjusts our bodily system to a normal function. Therefore, elimination is not unnaturally forced. Some experienced a more moderate process of elimination. Most patients sweat profusely. What I just stated explains why Taheebo is so effective and how it cures. Recently, a woman telephoned me complaining that due to Taheebo, she was going to the bathroom several times daily. Although she had been taking Taheebo for some time, this happened just recently. After considerable conversation, she told me that she had been taking estrogen pills as well, and this reaction happened only after she had stopped taking estrogen and was on Taheebo tea only. Therefore in her case, estrogen, in some way, had impeded the proper work of Taheebo tea.

I consider myself lucky, in that my tumour was where it could be easily expelled, without doing any harm to me. I cleansed through the skin too. For some time, my entire body was covered with skin pustules. This didn't disturb me because I knew that in this way the blood was cleansing itself too. Therefore, elimination through the stool should be optimal, and every other way has to be open to avoid any complication.

My voyage to Europe was fantastic. I had no pain, and more than ever, I was convinced of my total healing. Arriving home in Dalmatia, I visited all the places so dear to me, which I had missed for so long. Somehow, deep down inside, I was afraid that maybe I would never come back again, despite my feelings and improvement in my condition. I spent much time with Mrs. Petra Fantov, the lady who had colon cancer similar to mine. As I mentioned earlier, at first I sent her Hydrazine sulfate, and it helped her. It would take too long to explain how Hydrazine works. It is quite sufficient to mention that it prevents cancer cells from using glucose and thus forces them to die by starvation. Regardless, it didn't develop into a major cure for cancer, although extensive research had been done on it around the world, especially in the USA and USSR. At the time that I found out about it, it was said that Hydrazine prolonged life expectancy in cancer patients by five or more years. When I had sent Taheebo to Petra, she was taking both Taheebo and Hydrazine together. She didn't abandon Hydrazine, although in that time I discovered that Hydrazine wouldn't cure her, and eventually the worst would happen. Later I found an article written about Dr. Joseph Gold, Director of the Syracuse Cancer Research Institute. He had been working with Hydrazine sulfate for 20 years. He used mild chemotherapy with Hydrazine. The National Cancer Institute and its Director, Dr. Vincent T. DeVita, opposed such research for a long time. The article says that such treatment can be successful only under the supervision of a highly qualified doctor. Other than Dr. Gold's experiments, no other success was registered. I suggested to Petra that she stop taking Hydrazine, and use Taheebo only, but in vain. In Taheebo she didn't believe.

During the day, I swam and sunbathed alot. In the evenings, I would visit my sisters, relatives and friends, still strongly believing that I would see them for the last time. Wherever I went, everybody was very kind to me. In every home they offered prshut (a special kind of ham prepared in Dalmatia), proshek (sweet wine made from raisins), and other specialties, but I never touched any of them. Instead, I ate various kinds of beans and vegetables. Although I felt fine, I didn't want to jeopardize my newly acquired good health.

Upon returning to Toronto, I went to see my doctor urologist. He was very pleased to find that my cancer had almost completely disappeared. A complete blood analysis was done. Except for the still noticeable scar on my rectum, everything else was completely normal. I didn't know whether the tumour was still active or not and examinations in that direction weren't done.

Persuaded by S. G., I went to see a Dr. homeopath. After a peculiar general checkup, he said that I still had cancer, but very small. The checkup he did with his secretary. She put one hand on my chest and another one stretched out. The doctor put some drops under my tongue and pushed her arm. Sometimes she endured his force, and sometimes she didn't. This signified to the doctor if something was wrong with me or not. He prescribed drops to be taken and said that within a month or so the tumour would be destroyed.

Six days before my next visit to the urologist, I went to see Dr. homeopath again. After another checkup, as described before, he said that I was completely cured. Six days later, complete tests done by my urologist confirmed this. At first I was seeing my urologist every month and a half, then every three months. After three years I was seeing him every six months, and now as a normal healthy person, I see him once a year. There has been no trace of tumours since.

HOW TO PREPARE TAHEEBO TEA

For preparation of Taheebo tea, distilled, or well-filtered water, which is free from heavy minerals, must be used. Lacking these, rain water, collected from the roof, is good enough.

Metal pots should never be used. Use Corning glass or similar utensils.

Bring one litre of water to the boiling point, then add Taheebo bark to the boiling water.

Boil it rapidly for 5 (five) minutes.

After five minutes, turn down the heat and simmer it for another 20 (twenty) minutes. All together 25 (twenty-five) minutes.

Allow the tea to settle down, and then strain it through a cheese cloth or paper coffee filter into a thermos bottle.

You may drink it hot, warm or cold. Taken hot is the best method. If it gets cold, it should never be reheated, but should be drank cold in that case.

Take a sip and keep it in the mouth as long as possible, so that it mixes with your saliva. This way the tea is absorbed by the mouth glands, and mixed with saliva, and when swallowed, is better absorbed by the stomach glands.

For any small type of health problem, one heaping tablespoon of Taheebo is a good dosage in a litre of water, and several litres per day must be taken. For serious cases more strong tea can be brewed. There is no restriction of how much or how strong tea can be taken. There are no side effects, or any damage from it.

NOTE: If taken during chemo-therapy or radiation treatment it might not work.

CHAPTER EIGHT

(EDUCATION
AND THE TWO SCHOOLS OF THOUGHT)

It would be wrong and unfair to conclude this book at this point. I owe much more to my readers. I have tried to describe my case in the best possible way, simply and sincerely. Curing cancer is not a simple thing. I may have dramatized my feelings. I did this on purpose, to tell my readers of the agony that I went through, what my thoughts were, what I felt about dying, and so on. It is important for all those who become terminally ill to know that we are all in the same boat, so to speak. I felt that it was very important to say a few words about that as well. I think, because medical science can't cure a person with cancer he or she is condemned to death. Despite what is said, chemotherapy is a killer. Radiation treatment has limited success, and can be as mutilating as surgery is. Surgery can be successful if vital organs are not affected. However, chemotherapy is usually suggested after surgery, to destroy cancer cells that may still be lurking in the system. Unfortunately, this only defeats the purpose of the surgery, as chemotherapy itself is a killer. I found Dr. Antony Sattilaro's story very interesting. He had cancer everywhere. Considering my own experience, and that of many others too, in 99 percent of cases, chemotherapy was recommended even though the cancer was localized. Dr. Sattilaro never mentioned such therapy performed on him, in either his article, or his book RECALLED BY LIFE. Why? He, as a medical doctor, knew that chemotherapy would kill him much sooner than undergoing no treatments at all; therefore, he didn't allow it to happen.

My wife was in the hospital with a woman who had breast cancer. Her daughter is a medical doctor in Belgrade, Yugoslavia. When her daughter heard about her mother's problem, she telephoned, saying: "Mother, take anything else except chemotherapy. I know that the doctors recommend it, but you are my mother. Although I am a medical doctor and disagree with my colleagues, you are my mother and I want you to stay alive". Naturally the doctors removed her breast, but because she refused chemotherapy and took Taheebo tea instead, she is alive and well now. Unfortunately, medical science doesn't consider any other cancer treatments other than the ones that kill off both the healthy cells with cancer cells.

To obtain success, a patient has to do many things. As you, the reader, might have noticed, I believed in my healing. This was the first step in the right direction. Secondly, I learned my lesson and stopped believing that doctors are Gods. I kept myself informed and refused to accept treatments that I knew in advance would hurt me more than I was already hurt. Most of the setbacks in my recovery happened because I was not informed enough, and accepted treatments detrimental to my well-being. It's true, I was ready to die; Therefore, I visited my dear ones in the old country, and said goodbye to my family. Although I never feared death, I couldn't afford to be unprepared. I was in a hurry to finish all the work I had in mind before my departure, but I never stopped fighting. I was decided to fight until the last breath.

Medical science could try to deny the way my healing happened. My doctors could say that radiation helped me. Dr. homeopath could say that the drops that he gave me helped. Then why did I have the same experience as those people described by Louise Tenney, through her research in South America and in the USA? Why didn't, what my oncologist suspected would happen, ever come about, when she gave me only one year to live? No doubt, she knew what she was talking about. She was talking from experience, which means that no such case had ever been cured before.

During my own healing process, I did everything to help others. Mr. Mun Yu, owner of "For Your Health" Health food store, and I became good friends. When I learned about Taheebo, I told him about my experience. Furthermore, I asked him to give my telephone number to anyone who needed information about Taheebo. I don't know if there is anyone unwilling to help others, but if there is, I recommend this spiritual therapy. There is no better satisfaction than the feeling that we have helped someone else. Mr. Mun did as I asked him to. Many people contacted me. Some benefited from my experience, and some didn't. It depended on how much they believed in it. As I will mention later, many cancer patients have difficulties in refusing medical assistance, despite how detrimental it can be. Since chemotherapy was mostly in question, all the help that they could have got from Taheebo or diet, wasn't good enough. Chemotherapy was destroying their system much faster than Taheebo could rejuvenate it. Not only did they not benefit from it, their conditions deteriorated.

It would be wrong to decline medical assistance altogether. If for no other reason than to control cancer and its development, we need it. As I stated before, our doctors are forbidden to treat us according to their consciences and abilities. They have to follow instructions received by the Medical Association, and therein lies their own and our problem. Despite the ineffectiveness and destructiveness of chemotherapy, radiation and surgery, they are nonetheless used. Because we have faith in our physicians, any sick persons and their families find themselves in a dilemma of making choices. We submit our lives to them, because we have no choice and then, through no fault of their own, they all too often deprive us of life.

Is cancer curable or not? From my own experience, and from that of others, I say without a doubt, cancer is curable, but we have to know how to cure it. Dr. Sattilaro cured himself with a macrobiotic diet, as did many others. From Louise Tenney's report about Taheebo tea, we can see that many were cured even when everything else seemed hopeless. We find that many prominent physicians cured cancer very successfully, as did many non-professionals such as myself. Usually it was a complete cure. Unfortunately, this information we won't find in medical literature. What we do find in these publications is that medical science cured some patients to a certain degree. I have always wondered how many people they cured completely. In his book RECALLED BY LIFE, Dr. Antony Sattilaro says: *"More than a million Americans are under treatment for cancer in any given year, while each year 700,000 more are being diagnosed as having cancer. The death toll of this disease is 400,000 a year and climbing. Meanwhile, the annual cost of treating cancer exceeds $20 billion annually. (He had written it in 1982.) Cancer has turned into the most frustrating, costly, and intractable disease humanity has ever known"*. Dr. Sattilaro is talking about the U. S. A. only, but on a worldwide scale, the numbers greatly escalate.

Again, there is no given number suggesting how many patients were cured from this disease. Removal of tumour-ridden organs is not a cure. If I had accepted what medical science offered, I would be dead by now. All they did was remove diseased parts, and offer little or no hope for full recovery.

Throughout my research, I came across documents and statements where many prominent physicians successfully cured cancer. Unfortunately, I learned that all those medical doctors were discriminated against, by the professional organization to which they belonged, and many of them also lost their license to practice. Whoever has read the book CANCER AND VITAMIN C, written by Drs. Pauling and Cameron, has noticed how careful they are in their expressions. The only wrongdoing of these conscientious doctors was that they understood that medical science is stuck in a dead end street, with no way out. These doctors conducted research on their own. They were led by logic that the body is its own best healer. They had great success in their research and cure of cancer. I was astounded to find out that they exclaimed in unison that cancer could be cured easily if only medical science wanted to do so. Some of them exclaimed: *"As long as more people live by cancer, than die of it, the cure for cancer will not be found"*. If this is true, then I am not surprised that Taheebo was taken off the market, the reason being, that many patients with cancer disease claimed that they were helped by it, therefore necessitating further research and reclassifying it from a food to a drug. This is a very noble idea, but how long will it take for research to be conducted, and what will happen to those in need meanwhile? How will research be conducted if it is banned? Can we believe that the Health Department will do anything under these circumstances? Taheebo needn't be withdrawn from the market. It must be used in hospitals with terminally sick people, this being the only way to prove its healing power.

Among cancer stricken people and anybody who are in one way or another affected by it, it is openly said that cancer has become a big racket. It is also said that the National Cancer Institute (NCI) and the American Cancer Society (ACS) in the USA, and the Canadian Cancer Society (CCS) have become too strong.

They have become a Government within a Government, and they are not allowing a cure against cancer to be found. Is this the truth?

In his book THE CANCER INDUSTRY, Mr. Ralph W. Moss, former legal aid for Memorial Sloan-Kettering Cancer Centre (MSKCC) in New York, sheds some light on the situation of a cancer cure in the USA. He says:

A CAT (computerized axial tomography) scan costs the patient $200.00 to $400.00. Physicians buy partnership shares in cancer clinical facilities, and then send their patients to be scanned there. Usually a doctor can earn 25 to 100 percent or more per year on an investment of $5,000 to $100,000. Those investments are generally open only to doctors. The more patients he sends, the more money his centre earns."

For example, a physician who bought partnership shares for $25,000 each in 1986 in an Elizabeth, New Jersey, scanner, received $10,000 profit per share in six months. That amounts to an annualized return of 80 percent, after just two years of operation. The venture's prospectus projects a total profit, after ten years, of nearly $250,000 per share.

According to Mr. Moss, the same situation exists with chemotherapy and radiation treatments. On the board of directors of MSKCC, ACS, NCI and others, are men from Chemical, Oil, Tobacco and other pollutant causing industries. Pharmaceutical Companies do not accept any herbal or chemical cancer remedies that are easily accessible and patentable, such as, Hydrazine sulfate, Antineoplaston, Laetrile, Vitamin C, and others.

Considering this situation, should we be surprised that Taheebo was pulled off the market? No, but why?! We must all ask ourselves why. Are our politicians doing all they can to advocate laws to protect citizens? If noneffective and degenerative medicine producers have the constitutional right to make profits, then the remaining citizens have the constitutional right to be healthy. Cancer is a nondiscriminating disease. The experience that I, and many others went through may one day strike those who prevented proper laws from being passed. In comparing cancer and all cancer societies, we find many similarities. The appearance and behaviour are identical. Cancer appears when our immune system fails. It spreads haphazardly, jeopardizing the well-being of our entire body. When the Canadian Cancer Society got the "green light" from the Canadian Parliament, and the American Cancer Society and the National Cancer Institute from American Congress, that is, when no control was put upon their activity, they became strong and thus ungovernable. No research can be done without their approval, and grants are given only to researchers appointed by them. Any alternate cancer cure is prohibited, although the "standard treatments" are more detrimental than beneficial. Billions and billions of dollars have been spent, yet nothing has been discovered. Why? Successful research thus far has shown that the immune system is in question. Bringing the immune system to a functional state means to cure not only cancer, but all possible diseases. It is easy to imagine what would happen, considering who and what is involved. Therefore, no cancer cure performed by our own body and its immune system can be allowed. Many have said: "When the American Congress, the Canadian Parliament and governments around the world introduce a law which will put tight control upon Cancer Societies' activities, we will have the cure for cancer the next day". I can't agree more. What kind of cure does medical science offer us? Surgery, radiation and chemotherapy are accompanied by mutilation, burning aggravations and poisoning, and in the end no cure is provided to cancer patients. Despite how curative radiation and surgery may be initially, they provide limited help. Chemotherapy, on the other hand, is just a killer. Surgery is often ineffective because when a tumour is cut, cancer cells may enter the blood stream, thus causing the metastasis.

At this point I would like to quote Dr. Gori, former head of NCI (National Cancer Institute): *"If you make an analysis of the people who have been on the National Cancer Advisory Board, for the last nine years,* you'll see that it's loaded with representatives of the big cancer institutions.

The President's Cancer Panel is one of these top-drawer groups. Its function is to inform the president of the progress of cancer research. Such people, smack in the centre of things, have wielded tremendous power over the direction of our cancer research policies for the past decade. They are oriented to, what some critics have called, the "magic bullet" approach: The belief that cancer can be treated like an infectious disease, and that some new drug - comparable to the antibiotics so effective in treating diseases caused by bacteria - will be developed to safely destroy cancer tumours."

This approach makes no sense with cancer, because tumours are the result of the body's own processes gone awry. Dr. Gori believes that cancer researchers should work towards finding ways of strengthening the body's immune system and straightening out its own metabolic processes.

"You don't try to kill the tumour selectively, but you try to increase the capacity of the organism to counteract the effects of the tumour. This kind of an approach has been singularly neglected by the establishment so far... I don't think they will find a cytotoxic drug effective against cancer. The odds against it are infinite, because the metabolism of the cancer cell is not very

different from the metabolism of the normal cell. The hope of finding a cytotoxic drug which is effective against the cancer cells but doesn't kill or damage the normal cells is a pipe dream. We've got to pay more attention to other approaches. Not only to the cure, but also to the quality of life of the cancer patient being treated. It's not enough to try to fight cancer, and forget we're treating a human being, in the process, often subjecting him to worse injury and trauma than is being inflicted on him by the cancer itself."

"I would hope," continues Dr. Gori, *"that we may be able eventually to bend the establishment into searching for new avenues... Even today,"* he stresses, *"there exist nontoxic therapies, well-grounded in scientific rationale, which are capable of greatly increasing the capacity of the body's own immune-defense system to counteract cancer (whatever its particular form), eliminate it, and restore the individual to health. Through such means,"* says Dr. Gori, *"the quality of life for cancer patients in this country could be improved in a practical way to an extent that would be unbelievable today."*

"I don't know," Dr. Gori says pointedly, *"if you've ever visited a chemotherapy ward where you see these youngsters with their gums bleeding, their hair falling out, full of bleeding lesions in their intestines that make it impossible for them to evacuate their bowels due to the chemotherapy they are getting. Their skin falls off, their teeth get loose, they vomit, they feel miserable - just because these drugs are so toxic. These cytotoxic drugs can and too often do cause secondary cancers to develop... It's not a cure, it's far worse than the disease."*

Dr. Gori also reveals a startling fact about the way many NCI-funded experiments are set up. He says that NCI cancer researchers are encouraged to choose subjects for their experiments based on *"play the winner"* policy. *"For conducting cytotoxic drug trials - later to be reported in the medical journals - the researchers take in only those (patients) who have the best chance of surviving."*

If all the above mentioned is true, then it is a deception to the public, and considering all the money spent for cancer research and its cure, we must do something to expose these lies and those who speak them.

I attended the yearly convention "Total Health", organized by Consumer Health of Canada. Many speakers, all medical doctors, spoke at length about the problems that I mentioned only briefly before. Some of them very strongly attacked the Canadian Medical Association for inadequate care for patients, especially those suffering from cancer. I met Jimmy Straus, a herbalist, the owner of *"Natural Way Herbs"* herbal store in British Columbia. He gave three lectures at the two day Convention. His lectures were the best attended, because they were the most interesting ones. When the crowd around him subsided, I approached him. He claimed that by an iris exam he could detect somebody's disease. When I asked him to see if there was anything wrong with me, he examined my eyes very carefully.

"You are completely healthy," he said.

When I told him about my case, he said:

"Joe, these days cancer can be cured as easily as the common cold, if we could only teach the public at large. You used one of many methods, and all of them are successful. It is a pity that all this is hidden from the public."

Describing my case, one can see that most of the time, I wasn't aware of what I was doing. I can't say that I knew what was good and what was bad for me. I explored, I read, I asked questions, I listened and thought. I did everything but panic. After the first bad experience with BCG treatment, I refused to undergo treatments that I suspected would be dangerous for me and would weaken my immune system and kill my appetite. Some things that I believed in, didn't help me. The combination of teas described by Maria Treben, didn't help me at all, but maybe with reason. When I started to use her method, it was too late because my bladder, after treatment with BCG vaccine, was covered with cancer. Maybe if I had used that method from the beginning, it would have helped. I considered many other remedies offered by friends and acquaintances. Vitamin C, a vegetarian diet, positive thinking and others. I went so far as to take the Silva method of meditation and obtained fantastic results. I considered every suggestion that I knew wouldn't harm me, despite the results. Mrs. Stefica Sestak suggested the use of garlic. I was already aware of its remedial powers. She suggested that every evening before bedtime I clean one clove of garlic, scrape it a little until the juice starts to appear, spit on it and push it into my rectum. The tumour in my rectum was very low (my doctor could exam it with his finger). If garlic is so good against infections, I thought, it would help me more than anything else, and probably destroy cancer too. I had nothing to lose. When I started this remedy, large pimples appeared all over my body. This was a positive sign that the garlic was working. It was absorbed through rectal glands into the liver and was expelling toxins through the skin. I used garlic in this way, on and off, and the result repeated itself. (I played my last card. Cancer would kill me or I would destroy it.) All this happened later. The change happened overnight when I started to use Taheebo tea. Everything else helped to some extent, but Taheebo won the battle against cancer.

When Mun Yu informed me that, by the decree of the Health Department, Taheebo had been taken off the market, I was shocked, to put it mildly, as was everybody else who had used it. Why had this been done?

"... Many individuals claimed that Taheebo helped them with many diseases, particularly with cancer. A Royal Commission will be formed to investigate it and reclassify it from a food to a drug," was the explanation given.

What a paradox! Despite the explanations given: That a Commission would be appointed to test it and reclassify it from food to drug, there was no plausible reason to pull it off the market. There are so many herbal teas on the market today. Why, then, wasn't Taheebo treated like the rest of them? If we had some other proven cancer cure, such an act could be justified. Therefore the move is simply absurd. Taheebo cured me from cancer, and nobody can deny it. I am thankful to Dr. oncologist from Princess Margaret Hospital for her honest opinion that I had only one year to live. This is what medical science offer to patients in similar situations. Naturally, when my situation changed, she couldn't believe it was happening. She had never seen such a case, because there were none. The change happened shortly after she had given me the death verdict. Dr. urologist had given me another assurance saying that something that I was taking was helping me. This is the reason to believe that Taheebo alone healed me.

By withdrawing Taheebo from the market, a great injustice was done to all cancer patients. Furthermore, this act has denied our constitutional right to be healthy. The words stated earlier in this book, that "as long as more people live from cancer than die, we will have no cancer cure"; in other words, the profit of some is more important than the health of many, seems more truthful than ever. Eventually, and the statistics speak clearly, many of those who are denying a cancer cure, will experience the same tragedy. Or perhaps, there is a cure, but reserved only for them?

Why is chemotherapy still used? Isn't there enough proof that it has killed all those who consented to it? Where is the proof that Taheebo killed anybody? There is none! It may be a rightful suspicion that it has no healing powers, that it works only as a placebo effect, yet again, the decision for withdrawing it from the market can't be justified. Besides, when we speak of placebo, we talk of the remedy without any curable or other value. When we speak of Taheebo or any other herbs, they have some value which are stimulating our system, without involvement of mind.

In 1988 I visited my family physician for a regular checkup. The mail had just arrived, and he was opening it while talking to me. At once he started to laugh loudly.
"What happened?" I asked.

He passed the letter to me. It was a letter from the Toronto Hospital saying that he was required to send a detailed report of when and how I had died. Of course he sent that report, informing them that I was alive and in good health. Did they call me to find out what had happened to me? To ask me what I had done if anything, to cure myself? To find out if the same method could be beneficial to other patients too? No! They are not interested in that. My case won't be registered in medical literature, because I wasn't cured by their standards and with their methods. Several times my urologist tried to use my case in favour of radiation treatment, speaking to his young colleagues practicing under his supervision, but I stopped him right then and there, after which he remained silent. I am ready to defend Taheebo herb to the last breath. Why is all this happening? I have clearly stated the reasons thus far in this book. Taheebo rejuvenates our immune system and this is dangerous to the medical practice. Therefore it is ignored, and millions of people are dying from cancer, needlessly.

At this point I would like to talk about something that I was afraid to talk of before.

In November 1990, when my manuscript was translated from Croatian into English, I sent one copy to my urologist. In my modesty and naivete I believed that he would be glad about what I said in my manuscript. Instead, he was displeased. I was flabbergasted. What was the problem? He didn't like what I said in my manuscript, and he wanted me to change it.

"No," I said. "What purpose would it serve to write a book withholding important information or giving wrong information to the readers?"

"I will take you to the court," he said.

"No you won't," I replied.

"What makes you think so?"

"Because I won't mention any names in my book."

"You are right. In that case, I can do nothing about it," he replied. "How could you say that medical science sentenced you to death and you had to choose which way to die, being burnt, poisoned or cut piece by piece? How can you say something like that?"

"Doctor," I replied. "Tell me what else do you do? If there is anything else, I would be more than glad to put it on paper?"

He was silent about that, then he asked.

"How can you talk about chemotherapy? You never had a treatment, and you are not a doctor enabling you to talk about it correctly."

"Doctor, forget what I know or don't know about chemotherapy. Others have said enough about it. Read the book CANCER AND VITAMIN C by doctors Cameron and Pauling. Besides, these are not my words. They are in quotations and in italics. These words are from a very noted American oncologist, Dr. Gory."

Again, he had no argument. The third question was his crucial and final one.

"How could you say that your doctors didn't know what

they were doing from the beginning to the end?"

"Doctor, do you remember when I was laying on the cystoscopy table, waiting for the first BCG treatment. One of your students (my urologist is a Toronto University professor) asked you: 'Doctor tell us how this vaccine works for this case and why.' Your answer was: 'Don't ask me that question, because I don't know. I am told that this vaccine works for this case, and that is all I can say.'"

"No, no," he replied. "I knew everything that would happen from the beginning to the end."

I started to shake. I stood up looking at him with a menacing look.

"And you intentionally hurt me so much knowing that you were hurting me, and proceeded despite?"

Then I remembered events that we agreed on and he did something completely different. I was shaking all over my body in rage. I better stop here not mentioning what rushed through my mind. I thought about those who will need this information in my manuscript, so I calmed down and sat. That tense situation lasted for several minutes, then he asked me.

"Do you want me to check you over?"

I just couldn't believe my ears. This man hurt me so much. He was practically killing me, slowly and painfully. Now he asked me if I would let him touch me again. I was shocked.

"No," I said.

"I presume you will never come back again?"

"You are right. I will never come back again." I replied.

"If you ever need help, you know where to come, and you are always welcome."

I just didn't believe that I was hearing it right. Where are ethics? Where is human morality? After all this he asked me to trust him again?

Josip Gabre

"Doctor," I said to him, "not you or any doctor will ever again put a hand on me. If I am ever in the same situation, I would die first. Do you believe that I was tempted to commit suicide so many times?"

"Yes I believe it," he said.

"Do you know why I didn't commit suicide?" I asked.

"No I don't know," he said.

"I didn't commit suicide because I believe in God. I believe that with this life He gave us all these problems and we have to carry on as it is His will. To take one's own life would be the worst sin possible, and I wasn't ready to commit it."

When he walked me to the door, he gave me a piece of paper saying.

"This is a good friend of mine. He is dying of cancer. We can't help him. I believe in Taheebo but I can't use it. Please, help him."

As soon as I arrived home I made an extra hard copy of the manuscript, called this friend and gave it to him. Recently I heard that he died. Naturally, he was surrounded by doctors, and probably never used Taheebo.

The next day I went to see my family doctor. I told him what happened the previous day and what had rushed through my mind.

"Better you control yourself," he said.

"Yes, I had better," I admitted.

I never went back to that doctor again.

CHAPTER NINE

(BY WELL-PLACED FAITH AND NOT FEAR ARE YOU SAVED)

Many people helped me in my war against cancer (Dragica Donia, Vickers Head, S. G., Stefica Sestak and others). They all supported me and encouraged me to endure until the end. In this same way I have tried to help others. This was the main motivation for writing this book. Here, in a simple way, I have tried to explain what is happening in the mind of a terminally sick person, what is going through the mind of his family, relatives, friends and physician. I can't emphasize strongly enough the danger of fear. Fear, because death is imminent and medical science cannot prevent it. We know there is no hope for us, therefore, we are terrified. That same fear pushes us to accept a cure that will lead us to the grave. We reach for that last straw, although we know there is no hope for us. This situation prevents us from turning to other directions for better and more effective help.

Firstly, every cancer patient has to conquer fear. Fear subdues our subconscious mind and thus forces our mind to work in a negative direction. Our metabolism malfunctions, and our system starts to work erratically. When we add to this malfunction all the various kinds of toxins that we consume everyday, we overburden all our organs, especially the eliminatory system, causing the immune system to fail and thus causing cancer. To reverse the situation we have to overcome fear. We must relax, and in doing so, concentrate on healing. Do we believe in God? If we do, then why fear death? If we believe in God, we have to realize that we are here for a short time only, and for a certain purpose too, after which we return home, to God and to eternity. If we fear death, then there is something wrong with our faith, or something is wrong with our conscience and we have to do something about it.

Secondly, every patient has to find the reason, why he or she developed this disease. In our system some disorder happened and there has to be an explanation. The first step towards our healing is finding this reason and correcting it. We can't expect to get better if we constantly poison ourselves, regardless of the cure used. With other ailments we could probably treat the symptoms and get well, but with cancer we cannot. Unfortunately, when our immune system fails, the symptoms are evident but the cure is not. Medical science is only treating symptoms, but as for the diseases, there are no remedies. Our immune system has to be brought to a normal, functional state; therefore, we have to eliminate the condition that damaged it. When we eliminate the causes that have damaged our immune system, we will have taken a big step forward in our healing.

Thirdly, we should never accept a cure that destroys our system. Destroying our immune system even further, makes no sense. We cannot cure ourselves that way. Cancer is a highly intelligent disease. It is a product of our own body, the cell that possesses all human intelligence, and we cannot beat it in a primitive way. Just how intelligent cancer is, and how it protects itself against medicine, will be seen later when I describe one case history.

Fourthly, it is time that we stop believing in the omnipotence of our doctors. They can help us against other diseases, but not against cancer. When it comes to cancer, doctors are as enfeebled and confused as we are; therefore, we must scrutinize everything that they offer us. We have to insist that our physicians give us a detailed explanation about cancer, how it happened and how it has to be cured. From there, we will discover how much they know about cancer and how much they understand the cure for it. Yes, one may say: "What can I do if I know nothing about it?" That is a good question; therefore, we have to research a little through literature and find out for ourselves. Our life is at stake, and we have to protect it. If we are not satisfied with our physician's answers, we have to dismiss them at once, and find others, better informed.

I did my best to describe at length how I cured myself. Others could have done the same but didn't because of their lack of encouragement, and because they did not believe it possible. I described Dr. Sattilaro's case to emphasize that more than one cure for cancer exists, despite common beliefs. Many have cured themselves by meditation. Our brain is a very powerful tool at our disposition. Through it we think, create, imagine, feel, remember, experience and dream. Our brain has created wonders on this earth, and it can do the same within our own system. I must emphasize though, that meditation may not work for everybody, especially when in a crisis, for meditation requires practice, and with cancer one has little power or time to learn. I heard about a man who cured himself after having eaten a bag of onions. Another cured himself by watching comic video tapes for weeks and laughed his cancer out of his system. Through the Silva Method I heard about a submarine commander who, during meditation, imagined cancer as an enemy battleship, and fired torpedoes at it.

In this book I have described how I cured myself with Taheebo tea. I gave information about a macrobiotic diet, which is another way to fight cancer, but that is not all.

RUDOLF BROJS METHOD

Rudolf Brojs, a well-known natural healer, cured over 10,000 cancer patients with a hunger diet. According to his explanation, our body, when depleted of albumen, eats everything in the system, all impurities including cancer. His hunger diet lasts for 42 days, and during that time the patient has to drink one quarter to one half litre of juice made of: 3/5 beet juice, 1/5 carrot juice, 1/5 celery juice, 1/15 of white radish juice, (if the white radish is not available, black radish can be used), and 1/15 potato juice. The following is the method he used in his therapy:

1. Drink one half cup of kidney tea in the morning, right after getting out of bed.

2. Approximately 30 to 60 minutes after that, drink one to two cups of sage tea.

3. After another 30 to 60 minutes, take one sip of vegetable juice mixture. It shouldn't be swallowed at once, but kept in the mouth to mix with saliva.

4. After at least 10 to 15 minutes, take one to two sips of Geranium Robertianum tea.

All these herbal teas should be taken without sugar or any other additives.

Kidney tea has to be divided into three parts. The first part, as already mentioned, has to be taken first thing in the morning, the second part at noon, and the third part in the evening before bedtime, in doses of a half a cup or one third of the prepared amount, according to instructions.

Following Geranium Robertianum tea, take several sips of the **lung tea** or one full cup, and after that, at intervals of 10 to 15 minutes, **marigold** tea.

The teas are rotated, two to three teas, and after that, one to two sips of vegetable juice, then again three teas and one to two sips of vegetable juice, and so on until the end of the day. It doesn't mean that we have to spend the day with a cup in our hands. On the contrary, these instructions help the patient regulate the regimen in his own way, considering that from one tea to the other, or from the tea to the juice, 10 to 15 minutes (or more) have to pass. During the afternoon, the patient may feel an increased desire for the juice. If so, he can take up to 500 ml a day.

If the patient falls asleep during the day, we have to let him sleep until he awakens on his own, after which he will continue with the program. As was said earlier, 125 grams of juice daily are required for the therapy and healing. Greater quantities may be consumed at no risk.

The kidney tea is to be taken only for the first three weeks. After a pause of two to three weeks, it can be taken again for a duration of three weeks. The therapy is understood to consist of vegetable juice and the mentioned herbal teas only.

To satisfy the patient's thirst, it is recommended to drink as much Garden Sage tea as possible. These herbal teas are very important, and the more the patient takes, the better it is.

Taking these small amounts of liquid food, sip by sip, mixes them with the saliva and liberates the digestive organs from overwork.

During the therapy, the patient has to engage in activities to keep his mind off the sickness and food.

If required, other teas may be introduced to the therapy.

THE FOLLOWING ARE THE MOST IMPORTANT HERBAL TEAS

FOR THE CURE OF CANCER

1. TEA OF GARDEN SAGE LEAVES

PREPARATION: One level tablespoon of garden sage leaves put in one half litre of boiling water. **Let it boil for three minutes**, remove from heat, and after that add one pinch of St. John's wort, peppermint leaves and balm leave's mixture. Cover and let sit for ten minutes.

For gargling, pour hot water over garden sage leaves and let sit for ten minutes, (one pinch for one cup of water).

Garden sage leaves contain a great amount of etaric oils. For laryngitis, tonsillitis and sore throat, these oils are important, but as a tea, these oils should not be present; therefore the tea must be boiled exactly three minutes or more. In this way the oil is destroyed, and a vital element very important for all glands, bone marrow, and intervertebral disks is then released. The beneficial qualities of this herb are exceptional. With reason a Roman Scientist once wrote: "Why die, when in the garden we have sage leaves?"

Comment: If the tea is too bitter, the herb residues can be disposed of.

2. KIDNEY TEA

CONTENT: Shave grass 15 gr., Nettle wort 10 gr., (best to use spring nettle wort), Kontgrass 8 gr., and St. John's wort 6 gr. This amount is enough for one person for the duration of three weeks.

PREPARATION: Over one pinch of mixture, pour 125 gr. (four ounces) of hot water, and let it stay for ten minutes. Strain this into a bigger pot. On its sediment pour another two cups of hot water, and boil it for ten minutes. Then strain this into the bigger pot where both teas will mix.

Kidney tea must be prepared in this way because there are five elements that should not be boiled. By boiling, these elements are destroyed. A sixth element, flint acid, is obtained from the **sediment** after having boiled for ten minutes. Kidney tea must be taken **for only three weeks.** It must be taken cold, in the morning on an empty stomach, before lunch, and in the evening before bedtime, half a cup each time.

Kidney tea is recommended primarily during every inflammation and before surgery. A preventive three-week therapy can be used three times a year, but with an interval of at least two weeks between each time.

This kidney tea mixture can be used for the bladder and for the kidney alike, considering that they are connected.

3. GERANIUM ROBERTIANUM TEA

PREPARATION: Over one pinch of the mixture, pour 125 gr. (4 ounces) of hot water, and let it stand for 10 minutes. Drink this tea daily, sip by sip, no more than one cup a day.

Geranium Robertianum tea is essential for all kinds of cancer, especially if the patient has been radiated.

4. MIXED LUNG TEA

This tea contains much natural calcium and is recommended to all those with cancer.

CONTENT: "Male" and "female" Lance leaf plantain, Iceland moos, Lungwort, Ground ivy, Common mullein, and Meum Mutellina (botanical name). Over a pinch of this mixture divided into equal proportions, pour 125 gr. (4 ounces) of hot water and let stand for ten minutes.

Not all the herbs mentioned, had to be included in this prepared tea. The patient can drink this tea as much as they want - the more they take, the better.

MEASUREMENTS FOR ABOVE MIXTURES:

If the herbs are roughly ground, one pinch; if they are finely ground, one half teaspoon.

Rudolf Brojs warns that all those vegetables used for the total therapy must be organically grown. Over 40,000 patients were cured from cancer and other incurable diseases with this therapy. Those who deviated from this therapy and used conventional methods as well (chemotherapy, drugs etc.) had no benefit.

QUALIFIED SUPERVISION IS HIGHLY RECOMMENDED FOR THIS KIND OF THERAPY.

In his health reading, Edgar Cayce prescribed three bitter almonds daily, to prevent cancer. Also in the Edgar Cayce handbook, HEALTH THROUGH DRUGLESS THERAPY, he mentions a woman who cured herself with a grape diet and grape packs.

MATOL

Matol is another product on the market very beneficial to human health. Although it is said that it is a mineral preparation in a nonmedical base, analysing it we get a completely different impression. It is prepared by a special process of extracts of flowers, foliage, roots and barks of chamomile flowers, celery seeds, angelica root (archangelica), sarsaparilla root, dandelion root, senega root, horehound root, licorice root, thyme, passion flower, gentian root, saw palmetto berry and alfalfa.

Each ml. contains the following active ingredients:

potassium	(potassium citrate)	25.8 mg.
potassium	(potassium glycerophosphate)	.16
iron	(ferric glycerophosphate)	.09
calcium	(calcium glycerophosphate)	2.19
iodine	(potassium iodine)	.0015
magnesium	(glycerophosphate)	.84

Considering therapeutic properties and traditional uses of these herbs, we know that they help us cure a variety of illnesses. MATOL supplies our system with 32% more oxygen, therefore alleviating us from digestive problems, aging, cirrhosis of the liver, anaemia, emotional and mental upsets, high altitude problems, prevention of wound infections, diabetes and others. How much it helps to fight cancer is not yet known, because research in that direction with MATOL, has not yet been done, but considering that it supplies 32% more oxygen than we normally receive, makes much of the difference. As Dr. Donsbach said, a higher intake of oxygen enhances our metabolism; therefore, according to the research of a group of medical doctors (Roman Catholic priests), as will be explained later, a higher content of oxygen in our system can prevent cancer from occurring, and attacks it where it has already occurred.

Up until now I have been talking about the cures for cancer. In most cases, when it is discovered, it is too late to do anything; Therefore, it is so important to prevent the disease. We live in very difficult times. Everything around us is measured in monetary value. In other words, to gain the greatest profit in the shortest time possible. With chemical fertilizers, we are depleting our soil of all kinds of nutrients. To give taste to our food, we put in additives which are exclusively chemical. Animals raised for food are injected with chemicals. These are all poisoning our systems. Poorly nourished organs have to work overtime to eliminate the toxins accumulated, thus causing them to break down. When this happens, we take other chemicals to cure the symptoms. Side effects may occur, and we take more chemicals to cure these side effects, and so on. If we ate organic food free of chemicals, we would be doing ourselves a big favour. Obviously we can't find everything that we want on the market, but at least we can supplement our food with natural vitamins and minerals, and/or anything else that our system requires which may be lacking in our food. Unfortunately there are more synthetics than natural supplements on the market, thus taking us back to square one with our problems.

CHAPTER TEN

(INCREASING YOUR OPTIONS)

The following chapter is dedicated entirely to an important and effective grass, the Green Barley.

Dr. Yohishide Hagiwara, a Japanese scientist, inventor and businessman, developed health troubles due to overwork and malnutrition. When his health deteriorated to the lowest point, he tried to restore it, first with synthetic remedies and when these didn't work, he turned to nature. After intensive research on over 400 kinds of plants, he came across the young barley leaf. He found it to be an extremely rich source of the broad spectrum of nutrients needed by the human body. He found that the green leaves of this embryonic barley plant contained the most prolific balanced supply of nutrients that exist on earth, in a single source

THE NEAREST THING THIS PLANET OFFERS TO PERFECT FOOD.

The juice is removed from young, fresh, organically grown barley grass - when it is richest in nutrients. The water is then removed from the juice at body temperature so that none of the nutrients are destroyed.

The resulting product is a powder containing a wealth of nutrients - vitamins, minerals, live enzymes, superoxide dismutase, chlorophyll, proteins, strong alkaline pH and other nutrients. It is blended with powdered brown rice - a rich source of vitamin B^1, B^2, nicotonic acid and linoleic acid.

It contains nature's balance of 16 vitamins and 23 minerals, all of which are in their raw, naturally chelated and ionized form.

It contains so much potassium that it has a diuretic effect, like "water pills".

As we know, there is no function in the human body that does not require enzymes or does not suffer if their supply is insufficient or absent. The juice from the barley plant contains several hundred types of enzymes corresponding to those found in human cells, and very high amounts of three especially important ones - SOD, P_4 - D_1 and Nitrate Reductase.

Dr. Mary Ruth Swope, in her book GREEN LEAVES OF BARLEY, says: Green Barley contains great amounts of superoxide dismutase (SOD) enzymes which in human nutrition fight the devastating effects of superoxides (free radicals). Superoxide radicals are oxygen molecules with an extra negative charge on their outer ring. This change in the oxygen molecules make it very unstable and with great force it bumps into other cells and tissues, causing great damage to the DNA and producing mutation (damaged cells). Therefore, SOD is a cell protector, a powerful free-radical scavenger. Furthermore, we know that P_4 - D_1 suppresses inflammation and stimulates DNA repair and stronger cell growth. We also know that 70% of carcinogens are nitric compounds, which is petroleum solvent, and that the enzyme NITRATE REDUCTASE acts as an antidote to these poisonous nitro compounds. Therefore, we have strong evidence that Green Barley should be a good cancer combatant.

In her book, Dr. Mary Ruth Swope published 127 letters from people who got well with Green Barley for various problems, such as:

ABDOMINAL CANCER
ALLERGIES
ARTHRITIS
ASTHMA
BACK PAIN
BACK AND LEG PAIN
BLEEDING GUMS
BLOOD PRESSURE
BREAST CANCER
BRONCHIAL ASTHMA
CAFFEINE ADDICTION
COLON CANCER
COMPLEXION PROBLEM REITERS
CONGESTION
CRIPPLING ARTHRITIS AND PAIN OF THE SPINE
DERMATITIS
DIABETES,
DISC DETERIORATION
EMPHYSEMA
EXPRESSION
FATIGUE
FLU
GOUT
HAY FEVER
HEART PROBLEMS
HIVES
HYPERTENSION

HYPOGLYCEMIA
INTESTINAL CLEANSING
LEG CRAMPS
LIVER CANCER
LOSE TEETH
NUMB AND TINGLING HANDS
OAT CELL CARCINOMA
OVERWEIGHT
RECOVERY FROM CHEMOTHERAPY
REDUCING CHOLESTEROL LEVEL
RESPIRATORY PROBLEMS
RHEUMATOID ARTHRITIS
SINUSITIS
SORE THROAT
SYNDROME ARTHRITIS
TENDONITIS
VARICOSE VEINS
and many others.

Dr. Swope documented most precisely the function of Barley Green and explained how it works. Information on how to order this book, which I highly recommend, is found in the index.

In 1986 I had been taking Green Barley for some time until I lost contact with my supplier. Of course, I was healed from cancer then, but knowing the nutritional benefits of Green Barley, which supplements us with minerals, vitamins and enzymes so badly needed for balancing our system, I wanted to continue taking it. I have now found other suppliers and am pleased that I can continue taking it.

I was happy to find Green Barley so nicely documented. Comparing it with Taheebo, I feel that there are many similarities between the two. Although Taheebo is not, or at least I haven't discovered it yet, as well documented, it has therapeutic power, different from that of Green Barley which is the complete food. Green Barley is able to balance our metabolism, helping the body to free itself from all kinds of toxins accumulated due to bad nutrition and different pollutants, thus reinforcing our immune systems.

As the reader has probably already realized, taking Taheebo and Green Barley together could benefit us immensely, and thus restore our health.

If we analyse all the remedies used by different people to combat cancer, we will see that in all these cases, in one way or another, the patient triggered their immune system and when restored, took over and led the battle against cancer. In all these cases faith played a very important role. Even our own physicians wouldn't be very successful in helping us with the simplest disease if we wouldn't believe in them. Therefore, no matter what method we use, we have to believe in what we are doing. No one should expect to be cured overnight. We contracted the disease over a long time; therefore, it will take time to correct it. Any remedy, despite how effective it can be, will work more quickly for some and more slowly for others. Therefore, we have to be patient, and display great faith in the healing process. Trusting in your best judgement and believing positively in your personal health decisions, will create this strong faith which enables healing to occur.

CHAPTER ELEVEN

(INTELLIGENT CELLS)

I met Desa right after her surgery. She had cancer between the rectum and the uterus, a very difficult position for successful surgery. After surgery, chemotherapy was prescribed, in the hope of solving the problem that the surgery couldn't. Right after surgery she started to take Taheebo tea, but without success, due to the chemotherapy treatment. Her condition got worse every day. To understand this case, prolonged scientific research would be needed because her case was a very peculiar one. For example, after every treatment she was very sick, but her hair didn't fall off. I wasn't surprised that she had problems with her stool because I had an elimination problem as did everybody else in this kind of situation.

Sometime later she asked for my advice. What advice could I give her? I am not a physician and I can't speak with any authority. I have my own experience and that's all. If I were a physician, perhaps I could do so, but in my position I just couldn't. I told her what I wouldn't do in a similar situation, and that was, take chemotherapy.

"When I asked my family doctor about it," she lamented, "he said that it is up to me."

"Of course," I said. "Obviously he can't tell you anything else if he doesn't want to have any negative consequences. That is the only logical answer, because as a moral person, he can't allow himself to suggest chemotherapy, and he can't allow himself to dissuade you from taking it."

I knew that chemotherapy wouldn't help her. Instead, it would push her quicker and closer to her grave. I gave her my opinion, for that was all I could do. I understood her very well and knew what she was going through. The difference between her case and mine was that I preferred to die if I couldn't get well again, but she had small children, and she wanted to live for them. After that conversation, something happened. When I phoned her four months later, she was a totally different person. Her voice was happy and full of vitality.

"What happened, Deso?" I asked.

"Nothing. Everything is O.K., Mr. Gabre," she said.

"How do you feel?" I asked, a little surprised.

"Fantastic!"

"Fantastic, how is that?"

"Well, I refused to take chemotherapy any longer. I drink Taheebo tea and I feel better than ever. Tomorrow I am going to the old country and I will be there all summer."

I was sitting in for Mr. Loncaric on his radio program "Sounds of Croatia", for two weeks. On Monday February the 1st, 1988, I picked up the mail on my way to the radio station. There was an invitation to attend a lecture about cancer, to be held by Mr. Barry Lynes the next day. That day and the next, I invited my listeners to attend the lecture. Desa's husband, Miki, came. He told me that Desa was in very bad shape. We had no time to talk that evening, but it was obvious to me what had happened. When she had stopped taking chemotherapy and went on

Taheebo tea only, she flourished. Desa had never told her doctor about Taheebo tea, so he was convinced that her recovery was due to the chemotherapy. Unfortunately, upon her return from the old country, he convinced her as well. She underwent chemotherapy again, and soon her condition worsened. Sometime later I received a telephone call from Miki. He told me that Desa had passed away.

Earlier I mentioned how intelligent cancer is, and promised to explain it. Cancer manifested its intelligence in Desa's case. This is how her oncologist explained it to her husband.

According to her oncologist, cancer barricaded itself against chemotherapy with cells that it produced. Chemotherapy couldn't reach the tumour, but devastated the rest of her system.

In Louise Tenney's report, on cancer's protective casing, Mr. Millin, the importer of Taheebo to Canada, mentions how Taheebo breaks that protective casing. Dr. Mary Ruth Swope, in her book GREEN LEAVES of BARLEY, repeats and explains further this phenomenon.

In the beginning of this book I noted what doctors Pauling and Cameron said about cancer. They explained precisely what is happening within our organism, and how cancer occurs. Although healthy cells and cancer cells are a product of our body, there are differences. Our immune system not only protects our healthy cells, it destroys cancer cells. We can compare this situation with that of our society. The peaceful and productive citizens require protection by our judiciary system and the police force. Crime, and especially organized crime (with which we can identify cancer), needs no protection. Cancer builds its own protection, wherever and whenever necessary. At first, chemotherapy kills both, cancer and healthy cells. The immune system which is weak, (otherwise cancer wouldn't occur) is now destroyed and the body is left without protection. Although chemotherapy is a foreign body, our system has no protection against it. This is not true with cancer. It encloses within its own protective enclosure where chemotherapy cannot reach it. Cancer cells contain too little catalase, and unlike normal cells, they are anaerobic, meaning that they do not require oxygen to be transported by the blood. They gain energy to metabolize within their own cells. This explains why chemotherapy cannot reach cancer and is exactly what Desa's oncologist explained to Miki in simple words. Although our immune system is cancer's principal enemy, cancer doesn't recognize it as such. Cancer doesn't build the protection against it, because the cancer cell and the healthy cell are both products of the same body and only our immune system can kill one and spare the other, selectively. In other words, a healthy immune system is very important in breaking down cancer's protective casing and ultimately destroying it.

This proves further just how detrimental chemotherapy is to our body. Medical science has been very well aware of this for a long time, yet it continues to use it. Of course, chemotherapy destroys some loose cancer cells that escape during surgery, but this is certainly not enough. According to doctors' Cameron and Pauling theory, if we would submit, even the healthiest human to chemotherapy, he would develop cancer. We already know how this process works. Chemotherapy wouldn't prevent the creation of new cells; therefore, newly created cancer cells would immunize themselves against chemotherapy and good cells would be destroyed.

Would Taheebo do a better job here? According to Louise Tenney's report, Taheebo rejuvenates healthy cells, including immune ones; therefore, Taheebo would build up the immune system and activate it against cancer. In other words, it would break its protective casing, allowing catalase to happen, and thus destroying cancer. It is imperative that extensive research be carried out in reputable research centres for Taheebo. Only in this way can Taheebo be judged accordingly. Therefore, considering what Louise Tenney said about Taheebo, I must believe that with Desa, Taheebo could have helped her, as it did before her physician convinced her otherwise.

Medical science is very well aware of how cancer spreads and of the mechanism involved. Every time chemotherapy is applied, the result is known, but widely ignored. Cancer barricades itself while chemotherapy is in the system, untouched. It is in a resting position, or, in medical terminology, it is "arrested". If the patient dies during chemotherapy treatment, it means that some vital organs are damaged by chemotherapy. When the treatment stops and cancer senses its absence, it opens up and attacks the whole human system. This in medical terminology is called "metastasis". In both cases we can say that chemotherapy was detrimental to the patient. Therefore what can we say about Desa? All I can say, is, she was only one in an endless death line, sacrificed to serve somebody to prove something impossible, which is, chemotherapy can cure cancer.

If we analyse all that is said about cancer treatment, especially what Dr. Gori said: *"we cannot kill cancer selectively"*, the battle is unjust. In other words: *"we cannot drop an atomic bomb on a city if we want to eliminate organized crime, because the criminals will be deeply entrenched in atomic shelters, while innocent, hard working people will be annihilated."* That is exactly what is happening when we treat cancer with Chemotherapy. Healthy, good cells die while cancer cells get away, untouched. These facts are very well known to the medical science profession, but for some reason they ignore them.

I am not saying that we have to ignore our physicians; not at all. They have the ability and the knowledge to do check-ups for us. But, for God's sake, let us kill cancer the natural way, as God intended, and not in a way that ultimately deprives us of life.

I was lucky to have had a physician who was never offended when I refused therapy that he recommended. Today, I strongly believe that if I had no BCG treatment, I would still have my bladder. Who is responsible for this? I cannot point my finger at any particular person. The whole system is responsible because my physician had no better treatment to offer. If I had Interferon after surgery, the consequences would probably have been the same as that with chemotherapy. Perhaps I would have had the same results as I had with BCG, because not much was known about Interferon then. What I learned about it much later, convinces me even more.

I can't really imagine the connection between cancer and viruses. There is no proof that viruses, discovered in tumours, actually cause cancer. Science in fact has no valid proof for this theory. Can we blame physicians when they suggest to patients that they undergo a therapy that they know in advance would be of no benefit? Perhaps, ... I am not sure. If they have no other choice, and they are forbidden to do differently, then the blame cannot be placed on them. As we do, they also believe in what they are told to believe, and they are unable to conduct research at their own expense. We have seen that a physician cannot even suggest to his patient what he feels is a better cure, because he is afraid of the consequences. Then where is the blame? If we consider the statement of many scientists liberated from the fear of consequences, that cancer is not curable because more people live through it than die of it, then it is obvious where the blame should fall. When cancer is no longer the lifeline to big profits to all those who produce ineffective drugs and machines to fight cancer, the cure for cancer will be found very easily. If this is true, and I have no reason to doubt it, where are our constitutional rights to achieve this end?

On the 10th of April 1990, an Italian lady phoned me. Her husband had prostate cancer. He had already undergone chemotherapy and much damage had been already done to him. She asked me if Taheebo would be of any benefit in his condition.

"Maybe not," I said, "because the toxins left by the chemotherapy were much too strong for Taheebo to have any effect."

She told me that he had to sign a paper allowing the doctors to test a new kind of chemotherapy on him. I asked her if the doctor had ever signed a paper saying that he would get her husband well.

"No," she said, "they don't do that."

"Haven't we heard terrible stories of experiments on human prisoners? Is that not the same thing? There, people were forced into concentration camps, and all their rights were taken from them. Here, by empty promises, we are lured to sign a paper, and to waive all our rights over our own body. What is the difference between the two?"

Naturally, Taheebo is banned because many people claimed that it helped them. But why is it banned? Here we have a straight answer; *it is inexpensive and it is healing, that is why.* If we allow cancer to be cured with it, many will lose their jobs, and many yet, their huge profits. In his book THE CANCER INDUSTRY, Mr. Ralph W. Moss documented that fact very convincingly. Cancer Societies and the Pharmaceutical Industry will not allow any cancer cure if it can't be patented, which in other words means that it can't be monopolized, and big profits can't be collected. I don't blame the manufacturers of these killing drugs, nor the researchers who are paid well to wander down dead end streets. I don't blame any of these for their lack of conscience for making and selling these drugs. Is not the manufacturing of arms the same as the manufacturing of ineffective and killing drugs? Millions are dying while few are making profits. What about the politicians; those whom we elected into office to take care of our affairs and to be on guard for our rights. They are here, very quiet and composed, failing to protect us helpless citizens, from an incurable disease. My declaration to them is: *Gentlemen, you will experience the same fate as we did when the pain takes over; terrible pain, with no words to describe it, known only to those who have experienced it. When your organs start to fail you, one by one, and death slowly approaches, you will think about the cruel decisions you made, but everything then will to be too late. If even these arguments can't awaken you, then it is useless to talk about human morality, conscience and consciousness. Then it is useless to talk in God's name and fend yourselves with prayers, because you commit the mortal sin called genocide.*

Through my research, reading everything I could get about cancer, listening to those suffering from it, I came to the simple but truthful conclusion; *Cancer and the Cancer Society are a mirror image.* Both of them appear the same way, behave the same way and have the same end result. In the society, the immune system failed and the Cancer Society became ungovernable. The same as the cancer within us, it eats our society and if we don't introduce stiff, governable law to control it, it will eat us to extinction.

In Time magazine April 25 1994, an article was published by the title "STOPPING CANCER IN ITS TRACKS". After I read that nonsense I wrote a letter to the Editor-in Chief. Here is that letter

JOSIP GABRE

4523 The Gallops
Mississauga, Ont. Canada L5M 3B3
Telephonr (905) 828 5845

Mississauga, Ont. May 18 1994

Mr. Jason McManus
Editor-In-Chief
TIME
Time & Life Building
Rockefeller Center
New York, NY 10020

Dear Sir:

In Time magazine of April 25 1994, pages 42 to 48 an article was published by the title "STOPING CANCER IN ITS TRACKS". As a cancer survivor, and author of the book, "HOW I BEAT CANCER", I have some comments on the mentioned article. Although the writer describes the cancer in detail, there is something missing, or wrongly interpreted. For example, the writer says:

"... To shield itself from patrolling immune cells, the cancer cells sprout spiny armour, like a sea urchin's..."

"... Until now, medicine has tried to overwhelm the cancer cell with brute force, slicing it out with surgery, zapping it with radiation or poisoning it with chemotherapy..." (my Italics and accent).

If all this just said, is true, I ask a simple question. How did humanity survive to the 21st century?

If we study our body functions, we will find just the opposite. The immune system is cancer's only enemy, and because it doesn't recognize it, has no defence aginst it. Cancer doesn't shield itself against our immune system. Truly, it defends itself against anything and everything applied from the outside, as chemotherapy, radiation, or any other, orally taken anticancer drug. These methods destroy the immune system and help cancer to metastasis. Therefore, the statement of your writer Madelene Nash, is wrong and misleading. Where is the explanation how cancer appeared in the first place? Creation of our cells has been known for a long time. Where is any word about that? How is it that cancer succeeds to avoid the immune system? What is wrong here? Is the immune system working or is it, for some reason, shut off?

What is our cell? Is there any difference from our cell and the human as a whole? What is the difference in organization between our society and those in our body within our cells? Your writer indirectly speaks about that. The impression is that we know everything, but the evidence is that we know nothing about cancer, or we don't want to know. I am not a scientist, and have no doctor degree, but one could contest that article, very easily, word by word, just by logic. What is happening in our society is not different from what is happening in our body or in the universe, for that matter.

My urologist, often said to me: "If I succeed to keep you alive for one year, I will cure you. The cure is just around the corner." That was ten years ago. Where is that cure? These new promises are the same as the old ones. Complicated explanations time after time take us further from the cure of cancer than we were before. Immune system is the key phrase. Let us rejuvenate it and get healthy. That is how I cured myself, and many others did as well. There is no money in this cure. Who will get sick ever again, when our immune system works properly all the time? What will happen after that? How many medical professionals would be pushed to the street? Our health, or lack of, is big business and cancer tops the list of money makers. That is our problem.

Josip Gabre

If you read the book, "CANCER AND VITAMIN C", by doctors Ewan Cameron and Linus Pauling, the chapter on chemotherapy, page 54, the first paragraph, you will find:

*"... **The chemical compound bis(2-chloroethil) sulfide, (C1CH2CH2)2S, commonly called mustard gas, is a deadly vasicant (blistering agent)... It was used extensively as a poison gas in World War I...**"* (my italics and bold).

Going back to your writer's statement, why do physicians split open cancerous encasing with brutal force? What happens to the rest of the unprotected cells? Analogous to this question, if we put two men in a room, one criminal and one innocent, hermetically close it and let in poison gas, what will happen? Normally, both of them should die because they have indentical metabolisms. But no, the cancer, criminal in our body, has a gas-mask, as your writer has described, and the innocent one hasn't. To believe that the criminal with the gas-mask will die and the innocent one, without the gas-mask will survive, is foolish. Just the opposite will happen. The innocent will die but the criminal will survive. Analogous to our society, sometimes criminals are protected and innocent people are punished and destroyed. Similarly, to eliminate organized crime in a city, should we drop the atomic bomb, in an effort to strengthen its immune system, the police force and judiciary system?

It is useless to make a story of what is happening within the cell, including misspelling of some DNA letters and so on. Give us the answer how to correct that misspelling. Where is our immune system? What role does it play in all this, what is happening, if anything? Beating the cancer from outside is so widely explained, but what happens to our natural defence force? Are we dealing with destruction only? Where is the healing part of the whole process? We kill cancer. We kill healthy cells. What is left after that? Don't you see how illogical all this is?

Enclosed, please, find my book, "HOW I BEAT CANCER".

Cancer is easily curable, but never with brutal force from outside. Our immune system which controls our health, when it fails for any reason, cancer and a host of other diseases, occur. Analogous to our society, when the police force goes on the strike, crime increases. This kind of article is detrimental to our society. Use of chemotherapy, for example, is a crime commited against humanity, and all those who use it, have to be persecuted and prosecuted. Either history will prove this sooner or later, and correct it, or we will slowly disappear from the face of the earth.

Sincerely yours:

Josip Gabre

Recently I received this answer:

TIME

Robert Cushing
Editorial Offices

Time Inc.

TIME
Time & Life Building
Rockefeller Center
New York, NY 10020

212-522-1212

July 7, 1994

Dear Mr. Gabre:

Thank you for writing in response to the April 25
cover story on cancer. We regret your feeling
that the report was at all off the mark, but we
certainly appreciated having the opportunity to
consider your thoughts on our approach. It was
also good of you to send us a copy of your book,
which has been circulated among the editors. Our
thanks, again, for your interest in our coverage,
and best wishes.

Sincerely,

Robert Cushing

Mr. Josip Gabre
4523 The Gallops
Mississauga, Ontario
L5M 3B3 Canada
RC:sf

CHAPTER TWELVE

(CASES UPON CASES)

K.C. and I had known each other for many years. She had colon cancer. After surgery everything was fine, but she didn't take proper care of herself. I warned her that she had to change her lifestyle completely, from what she ate to what she drank as well as her attitude towards life. She had to take care of herself because from one moment to the next her immune system could fail her again, and cancer would be back in no time. She hadn't eliminated the cause that had brought her to this condition. After a long vacation in Europe, she came back with a cold. She went to see her doctor, and the X-ray showed something. Because she had a cancer history, it was taken for granted that it was a cancer lesion. A biopsy was done and showed positive. Chemotherapy was recommended. I begged her to decline chemotherapy, but she had too much faith in the doctors. She was a wealthy woman and tried everything that modern medicine offered her. In vain, I tried to convince her to concentrate on Taheebo only. She found all kinds of excuses for not taking it. Of course, she died.

Interestingly, after the funeral, her daughter told me.

"Mister Gabre, my parents programed themselves how to die. My father was always terrified about heart attacks, and that is how he died. My mother always feared cancer, and as you can see this is the way she died."

Really, is that possible, that our mind can be so strong, it programs us to get certain diseases? I strongly believe it. We can program ourselves how to get sick, and when we get sick, how to cure ourselves. I did just that. When I found Taheebo, nobody could dissuade me that it was my cure.

Late one evening A.S., a good friend of mine, called me. That same day he had received a letter from home that his mother had cancer, and preparations were on to give her chemotherapy treatment. He knew my case and asked for advice. The medical facilities in the old country where she was being treated are not as they are over here. I knew that she had to cleanse herself because that is the main problem with cancer patients. It was grape season, so I suggested that she go on a grape diet. Only grapes and water, nothing else, for between fifteen and thirty days. I suggested that he call her immediately to prevent chemotherapy treatment. Within a couple of days he went there, and took with him Taheebo and vitamins, the same kind I had taken before. He did everything as I suggested. Four months after she started taking Taheebo, she went for a checkup and was found completely healthy.

Ralf was a salesman in a furniture department store. I was buying a reclining chair. He was so polite, and so helpful that I felt an obligation to do something for him. It was a feeling within myself. I went to the car to pick up one of my books and gave it to him as a token of my appreciation. Several months after that, he developed cancer. Having this information in the book, he used Taheebo accordingly and got cured.

Pasquale S. had stomach cancer. Three quarters of his stomach was removed, and the cancer was still there. His son kept me on the telephone for a long time with long lists of questions. When satisfied with my answers, he brought his father to me. Pasquale was in such bad condition that, I honestly doubted he would make it. He followed instructions from my book. After a month and a half he came to me, alone. There stood in front of me, a completely new man. Today, he is cured from cancer.

One gentleman from Oakville Ontario, phoned me several years ago. His doctor diagnosed him with lung cancer. He read my book previously, and refused chemotherapy or any other treatment, being ready to die. He phoned me and I explained to him what he had to know of cancer and its cure. Several months after that he was cured.

In 1992 one lady phoned me from Hamilton Ontario and asked me if Taheebo helped mental disease.

"I don't know" I said to her. "You have to try it, to find the truth."

That was in June or July. In December she phoned me to tell me what happened and to wish me a Merry Christmas. After approximately a month and a half she was proclaimed healthy by her doctors. Instead of being institutionalised she threw away all her pills and now enjoys good health.

It is difficult to say how many people used Taheebo and were actually helped by it. I am not a professional and as such I don't keep records. Many contacted me, and I did my best to explain my case, with the intention of helping them to make up their minds. I asked them to contact me and inform me about their progress. Few people are ready to share their experience with the intention of helping others. The following are examples of unconfirmed results lacking such documentation.

At the time that I was speaking about my experience on the radio, a Jamaican lady contacted me. She told me that she had fibroid. To be honest, I had never heard of this disease before, and I told her so. When she explained to me what it was and that medical science had only a surgical answer for it, I suggested that she try Taheebo. Even if it didn't help, it wouldn't harm her. She took Taheebo and after one week she went for an ultrasound test. Results were negative. I asked her to write me a letter about what had happened so that I could put her case in this book but I never received her letter.

After this another lady, whom I know very well, had fibroid which was removed surgically. The surgery however didn't improve her condition. After taking Taheebo for a short time, her problems disappeared.

There is too much aversion towards Taheebo and with good reason. To convince someone that the inner bark of a tree can successfully cure cancer, while medical science still can't find the cure for it with so much money having been spent on it, is the main stumbling block. It is very difficult to show where the truth lies when there is so much faith in the medical establishment. Therefore, only those with a little intuition and much courage have beaten cancer with Taheebo, as I have. There were those who took Taheebo but meddled with killing drugs simultaneously, and they had no success.

One gentleman whom I knew casually, phoned me. I explained what he needed to know about Taheebo. He had positive results within a short time and he phoned back within a couple of weeks. He annoyed me with questions such as: "Is it the merit of Taheebo that creates the improvement or is it something else?" At that time he wasn't taking anything else, and I asked him what else it could be, if not Taheebo. He asked me if smoking is dangerous, (he had lung cancer, due to heavy smoking). I explained to him how dangerous smoking is and suggested he never smoke again. Then he said that his doctor told him to smoke with no fear of damage. "Leave that doctor at once," I said, "if you want to get well." Of course, with such an attitude, he died. After his death I learned that he had been eating the worst foods possible, smoked more than ever and drank excessively too. He had stopped drinking Taheebo tea altogether. The result of this behaviour didn't surprise me at all. Suicide needs no further explanation.

One lady came to see me a year and a half ago. She was a medical laboratory technician. Listening to her, one would have the impression that she knew everything one had to know about cancer and its cure. Instead, she was the biggest ignorant I ever met. With Taheebo she was taking Esiak, and Shark cartilage in addition to undergoing chemotherapy. I asked her why she took chemotherapy and she told me that she wanted to have scientific proof of her improvement. She told me that if she didn't take chemotherapy, her doctor wouldn't give her tests. Of course, that was foolish, and I told her that with her attitude she wouldn't make it.

"Oh yes, I will make it. You see I didn't lose my hair and I feel so good."

"No, you won't make it," I said, "because you are confusing your mind, and that is the worst thing you can do to yourself."

She didn't succeed, she passed away.

At this point I would like to explain what is happening. If we take any number of herbs simultaneously, combining all of them in our mental process, it will work. Conversely, if we jump from one to the other, disregarding them accordingly, because they didn't give instant relief, we confuse our mind and nothing good will happen from that. Therefore, it doesn't matter what kind of remedy we take, we stimulate our body and our mind to work together and that is where the cure comes from, for any and every disease. This is what actually happens when we take the synthetic drugs which our physicians prescribe to us today. By believing in our physicians, we set up our mind toward healing, despite the fact that we are taking poison that cures only symptoms.. Even in that detrimental situation we feel better, only because we set our mind to that direction. From this we can understand how much more we can get from medicinal herbs that our system easily assimilates and eliminates.

While I write these lines, Daniela phoned me. Daniela, with her family, is a newcomer to Canada, from Romania. Several months ago she came to see me. She had cervical cancer and started to take Taheebo tea. A couple of days ago her doctor proclaimed her cured from cancer.

Talking about smoking, questions are entertained how dangerous smoking is, how much it causes cancer, and what kinds of cancer it causes. The general opinion is that smoking causes lung cancer only, but is it so?

At the convention "TOTAL HEALTH" in Toronto in 1985 a report was released by a group of Roman-catholic priests, all medical doctors. For 45 years, they conducted research, correlating the content of oxygen in humans with cancer occurrence. They found that our healthy cells and good bacteria, which we need for digestion, require large amounts of oxygen for their normal function. As mentioned before, they are aerobic. Cancer cells, and bad bacteria, which from the outside invade our system, need no oxygen at all. They are anaerobic. This is the same thing that we said before about catalase. From this we can draw one conclusion. Smoking is depleting our system of oxygen. Alveoli which enveloped by a network of capillaries load large amounts of oxygen into blood, which is distributed to the cells through our system. When these alveoli are damaged or clogged, due to smoke or air pollution, they cannot supply enough oxygen to certain organs, whose oxygen supply they control. The cells in these organs convert from aerobic to anaerobic, meaning from healthy to cancer cells. With other factors, it contributes to the occurrence of any kind of cancer, anywhere in our body. These priests devised a special formula of Hydrogen Peroxide for internal use only, and included instructions on how to use it. Hydrogen Peroxide increases oxygen in our body and not only cleanses our system, but kills cancer and eliminates its dead cells in many different ways. If we look at the properties of Taheebo, we will see that it is an ozoniferous plant. For Ozone we find this definition in Webster's dictionary and in Encyclopedia Britannica: *"Three atomic elements, the oxidizer, regarded as an allotropic form of oxygen, much more active than ordinary oxygen and completely clean from any pollutants"*. From this condensed definition it is hard to get all the answers that we would like to have, but, considering that it has a strong cleansing factor, it becomes clear why Taheebo has such strong cleansing powers that are very important for purifying our system of toxins that cause cancer.

Another cancer case occurred in my home. My wife Mladenka sensed an itching on her left breast, just a few days before our departure to Italy where our daughter expected to give birth to her first child. The specialist couldn't say that it was cancer, but just the same recommended chemotherapy. Of course I didn't allow this treatment, and we left for Italy. The oncologist in Como, Italy, came up with the same diagnosis. The biopsy showed positive, and chemotherapy was recommended again. I tried to reason with my family and convince them that Taheebo would cure her and to forget chemotherapy altogether. As I said earlier, what happens in such a situation. The fear prevails, and therefore I had no support. My wife had the chemotherapy and got worse every day. I prayed to God to help us get away from that negative influence, and get back to Canada as soon as possible. I have to mention that she didn't take Taheebo as I had recommended, and even today I can't understand why. Upon our arrival back to Canada, we visited oncologists and had no luck. All the top ones were on vacation and we happened to get to a very young doctor. He didn't want to consider anything less than a modified radical mastectomy, which in popular jargon means complete removal of the breast. Again I tried to reason with my wife but it didn't help. As I say to everybody who asks me for my opinion: if I were the one in question, I know what I would do. I can't make the decision for others, not even for my own wife. I wouldn't take chemotherapy or anything else, I would stick to Taheebo, and nothing else. My wife didn't listen to me again and had a radical mastectomy. After the surgery was completed, her doctor recommended chemotherapy again. That's when I blew my top. I had a nasty argument with her doctors, and forbade her to take anything but Taheebo. One of the doctors, of the three of them in the office, said:

"What if she dies?"

Hearing that I asked her:

"Can you put on paper that you will cure her, and sign it?"

"No, we cannot give that assurance to anybody", she said.

"Then keep quiet, please. What if she goes on the street and gets hit by a car? If her time has arrived, nobody can save her."

Then they suggested to my wife to take estrogen pills. I asked for all possible information about estrogen, before I allowed her to take these pills.

"We don't give anybody this information," one of them said.

Fed up with the whole situation I became very rude.

"No? But you will give it to me. Unless you give me this

information, I won't move from here. If you want to have a scandal, please, go call the police."

Of course, she went to her secretary and ordered her to collect all the information for me. Prescriptions were written and we bought the drug. After I read the information, I explained to my wife what it was and what she could expect from it.

"Do you want to take these pills?" I asked my wife.

"No," she said.

These pills ended up in the garbage, and never was that prescription refilled. Her doctors in W. C. H. thought that she was taking the pills, and we, naturally, never told them the truth.

When she went to see her doctor for a checkup I never left her alone. I know he hated me for that, but I couldn't allow her to be brainwashed again. I put her on Taheebo and saved her life. I am very sorry that I wasn't more forceful in the first place. Just the same, I saved her life.

My wife, as all women who had modified radical mastectomys, since the surgery, has a swolen gland under her arm. Her doctor tried to convince her to have it removed and I opposed it. I may be wrong, but from childhood I remember, whenever I hurt myself on the arm or upper part of the body, that gland swelled, and stayed swelled until the problem was gone. Because my wife has permanent surgical damage, in my opinion, that gland will be enlarged for the duration of her life, therefore I opposed any surgical intervention to remove it.

When I was sure that my wife wouldn't let her doctor brainwash her, I let her visit him alone. Lately she told me that he is still coercing her to let him remove that gland. On her last visit to this doctor I accompanied her. I wanted to know why he was doing that. I asked him simply:

"Doctor, can you tell me what it is? Is it a cancer or not, and if that is not a cancer why bother?"

He ignored me but in every way tried to convince her to allow the surgery, telling her how many women had undergone it. From his facial expression it was easy to see how unhappy he was that, after six years there were no lumps anywhere. I was just about to ask him how many of these women are still alive, but he abruptly left the examining room.

To all women with breast cancer I strongly recommend Taheebo. Since my book, in Croatian, has been on the market, many have contacted me with that problem, and all those who used Taheebo tea got well, unless they meddled with something else in the same time, such as chemotherapy, or something similar.

K. D. D. is a unique case. She wrote this letter to me, to explain her case for the benefit of others.

"In mid October 1990, I woke-up and discovered traces of a secretion that had come from the nipple of my left breast. I went directly to my family doctor who suspected the secretion to be blood. He sent me to a surgeon. A mammogram was taken and samples of secretion sent to a laboratory for further analysis.

"The lab confirmed my doctor's suspicion. The secretion was indeed blood that contained some dead cells. The presence of these dead cells suggested the possibility of cancerous cells in my breast. However, the cells were dead... or the cancerous cells, somehow, had been destroyed.

At this point, the doctors offered me two options: Operate on the breast to remove a small tumour or wait and see for further development.

I opted to wait. Two months later, the small tumour had disappeared and the secretion from the nipple did not recur anymore. The doctors informed me that about 2 out of 3 women with a similar problem, normally develop cancer of the breasts.

It is my strong belief that the regular drinking of the Taheebo tea has prevented the spreading of the cancer in my breast. The Taheebo tea has helped me often and I consider it as having been tremendously beneficial to me. Every fall, I was plagued by long and nasty bouts of flu. After beginning drinking this tea, I have never had the problem since.

Taheebo tea has helped me with my digestion and it is a very positive factor in speeding-up any kind of injury that I incur. As well, it seems to calm my nerves.

When I first began to drink Taheebo tea, I was afraid to become dependent on it. As an experiment, I stopped taking it for a whole month. The stoppage did not have any effect on me. Therefore, I started drinking the Taheebo tea regularly and I find that it has many beneficial effects on my well being."

K. D. D.

E.K. is a friend of mine. He had developed the same kind of cancer that I had. We even shared the same urologist. Knowing my case, he asked me for my opinion. I explained to him what happened to me, with the same BCG therapy that the same doctor recommended to me. He refused BCG treatment and went on Taheebo. After taking Taheebo tea, an improvement took place. But he went on a prolonged trip, stopped taking Taheebo during that time, and abandoned a proper diet. Cancer recurred. He became bitter. When I asked him how much Taheebo he took daily, he said: a cup or two here and there. That is not a proper way to treat cancer. We got cancer over a long period of time, abusing our system. In the same way, we can't cure it within a couple of days, and with a couple of cups of Taheebo tea, taking it now and then. To cure ourselves we have to drink several litres daily, and for a long period of time. Even after cancer disappears, we have to continue taking Taheebo until our immune system returns to a normal condition. Regardless, he went back on Taheebo and on a macrobiotic diet and is well today.

Mrs. M.P. phoned me when she heard about my book. With the book she ordered Taheebo, and another herb recommended for ulcers. My herbalist was very busy in those days, and she phoned every day, sometimes several times daily, lamenting that the herbs hadn't arrived. When she finally received Taheebo and had taken it for a week, she sent me a letter explaining her problem. It all started with simple surgery. Her doctors had given her pills that caused side effects. Another pill followed the previous one to cure the side effect and so on until she was taking forty-one different pills daily. She was completely poisoned with pills and her problem was mounting further. After having taken Taheebo for only one week, her symptoms started to disappear one by one, and she stopped taking pills altogether.

I. C. called me from Montreal and told me about his brother Mark, in Sisak Croatia (Yugoslavia), who suffered from throat cancer. I sent him my book and Taheebo. Three and a half months later, I got another call from Montreal. Mark was completely healthy again. He used the instructions from my book and Taheebo tea only.

Despite the ban, we can still get Taheebo. But this is not enough. It has been proven that it cures cancer and many other diseases; therefore, the ban against it has to be lifted as unjust, and allowed to be used by conscientious physicians, whenever necessary. A Royal Commission has to be appointed to investigate it, and to recommend it as a cure for cancer and many other deadly diseases. The way it is imported opens the door to all kinds of manipulation, such as a decline in quality, price fixing and others that could go against the interest of all those who need it.

April 22 1994 in the Globe and Mail, page A13, Miss Lisa M. Cherry published the article about the Emergency Drug Release Program (EDRP). She reveals in this article a long time law by which doctors can use nonconventional methods of curing patients. My urologist, apparently never knew this law. Strange, for a Toronto University medical professor, I thought. What does he teach his students? Regardless, he probably would never consider it anyway. Instead, he used a BCG treatment and destroyed my blader within three weeks. What happened after that, I was hurt more and more. If I didn't find Taheebo in time, obviously I would be dead now.

I hope that this book will reach the right people, not only cancer patients to help them, but politicians as well, to awaken their conscience and help them to understand the agony of all those stricken by cancer. Gentlemen! You, who are still healthy, remember that our health is the most precious treasure we have. We are very wealthy when we have it. Once we lose it, we can't gain it back. And when we lose it forever, what then? Who can say that he or she is immune to cancer, and will not experience what I and many others had experienced? Cancer does not discriminate - it affects everyone. Even famous people are dying needlessly; Jacqueline Kennedy is one of them.

Gentlemen, medical science has no cure for cancer. Why? Ask the Cancer Societies and Medical Associations. I tried to answer this question, and if you research yourselves through the libraries as I have, you will find the truth too. Put control on the Cancer Society. Put a control on the Medical Association. Do not let them monopolize our lives. Let so-called orthodox medicine compete with alternative medicine, and let it gain recognition in a fair way. Force them to get out of that dead end situation and look for a cancer cure elsewhere, because the cure for cancer does exist. Any postponement can cost you your lives. When that happens, you will be sorry, because it will be too late.

SVIJET (World) FROM SARAJEVO
BRINGS THESE REPORTS.

HOLY TREE CAN DO ALL OF THIS.

In this issue we reserved space for Taheebo, a miraculous tree from the Andes - "Holy Tree," as Brazilians call it. The following who were asked to tell us about their experience with the usage of this tea, came to the same conclusion. Mirsada Arifovic belonged to the group of people whom one would say is "bursting with health." This sounds unbelievable, but to this 34 year old lady from Semberia, until six months ago, it was unthinkable to even open up a health file on her. Last March, for the first time in her life, she developed a high fever. It occurred as though someone had "injected" this into her overnight. For days, the mercury in the thermometer never dropped for even a moment. It was over 37 C all the time. At the beginning, nobody was concerned about it. Even her coughing and sweating never concerned anyone. Then one morning, Mirsada could not move her arm nor speak. At the hospital, the concern was that she had tuberculosis. There was no improvement in her condition and additional tests were conducted. The final diagnosis was bronchial carcinoma. In Zagreb, the diagnosis was confirmed by a most respected medical doctor. With his findings, he cut the wings from her smallest hope. He said, that Mirsada had less than three months to live. Nevertheless, he decided to administer chemotherapy anyway. Not be-

Josip Gabre

cause he believed there was any hope for her recovery but more to satisfy her for having made the trip and seeking further help.

Upon returning home, Mirsada drank her first cup of Taheebo tea. That night her family gathered around her bed to watch her sleeping soundly. The following day Mirsada walked again and got colour on her face. She felt strength in her body. Crying with happiness, she said that she was without pain. Only a day before, pain was debilitating her and she was going out of her mind.

ASTOUNDED DOCTOR

Her doctor couldn't believe it. The tumour was shrinking! He was no less surprised when his patient told him that she did not feel any of these happenings following chemotherapy. Then, in Zagreb, Mirsada received another dose of cytotoxic. We spoke with her several days after that, with our fingers crossed. She says that she couldn't explain why she never told the doctor about Taheebo, which she was drinking instead of water. *"Perhaps I was a little afraid that I would hurt his feelings. How could I believe more in herbs than in my doctor?"*

Of Zorica Vukovic, who now sleeps confortably after two years of insomnia.

"I was tired, lethargic, indifferent to everything around me. I was waiting for some disaster to occur from within. I accepted Taheebo as a solution for myself. The first and second night I didn't sleep. I didn't sleep the third night either. Regardless, I didn't abandon the Taheebo tea because I noticed other things happening, as though some weight had been lifted from my shoulders. The fourth night I sank into a deep sleep, and in the morning I woke up feeling fresh, relaxed and in some wonderful way, cleansed. One month already and I have never taken one pill. I can't recognize myself..."

Vera Mitrovic also from Sarajevo, is 61 years old, and had already been on the surgical table eight times. She can't even remember how often she was in the hospital. The last time was less than a month ago, because of blood pressure that was hovering around 270/140. Each week, her doctors changed the treatment and each time they shrugged their shoulders.

DESTROYED HIGH PRESSURE

When she left the hospital, Vera tried Taheebo. The reaction was strong; her high temperature was substituted by shivering constantly. Twice she had diarrhea.

"Somehow I pulled through after that. My condition improved and is continuing to this day. My blood pressure is much lower (180/114), although I no longer use pills, (which I previously used every second day). There is no swelling on my body, nor unbearable pain, below my rib cage. I am not waking up overnight as I used to, and I am more calm and relaxed."

When Borka Markovic in May of this year appeared on the doorstep of her parent's home, her father and mother couldn't believe what they saw. Instead of seeing their daughter who was always well rounded, there was this frail skinny, young woman. All that was visible on her pale and ashen face was her big green eyes. Borka's husband worked in an African country, where social security is nonexistent, and where complicated surgery was unheard of. The Sarajevo woman never questioned whether surgery was necessary. A section of her stomach with an ulcer had to be removed. She lost weight, 15 kilos. At the Kosevo hospital, the doctors decided to operate but they found cells that were suspicious.

149 *Josip Gabre*

The entire family panicked. A friend of theirs from Beograd made an appointment with a noted specialist in intestinal problems. Ten days later Borka appeared in his office. The examination confirmed that her condition was not alarming as she was advised. What was happening?

SURGERY NOT NECESSARY

"Just two to three days after that, pain completely disappeared, and along with it the vomiting and belching disappeared as well. Then I felt hungry and started to eat foods that I avoided for years. First, egg. Nothing happened; then watermelon, and again nothing happened. I drank one beer. Again nothing happened. On my plate there were greasy, hot and sour foods and I had no problems with it. I related this to the doctor in Beograd, who suggested that I continue taking Taheebo tea, and he recommended another appointment."

A month later, a gastronomy exam showed that the ulcer had disappeared.

"Surgery is not necessary," concluded the doctor who then asked: *"What is the name of that tea?"*

Rada Tosic from Sarajevo started to drink Taheebo tea twenty days ago. Her experience is even more interesting because she is a medical worker: *"Every day I had terrible headaches. Now I don't have them. I have no dizziness either, which I had always. I have no heartburn, which disappeared suddenly. Also, my brother started to take Taheebo. He was just released from the hospital for pancreas problems, where he spent seven days in intensive care. Laboratory analysis showed his condition as excellent, which is not customary after problems such as he experienced, and not after such a short time..."*

WHAT PATIENTS SAID ABOUT TAHEEBO

REMEDY OF SWIFT EFFECT

SLEEP

Seven months ago Nezir Kadic was diagnosed: cancer on the bronchi. Since then he spent one month in hospital, and one month home, rotating endlessly.

When we spoke with him, he had been drinking Taheebo for five days: *"The next day I already noticed that I had no high temperature, which had plagued me all this time. That also made me feel tired and lifeless. Since I took Taheebo for the first time, I sleep very well. Today for the first time I walked to the doctor's office. Prior to that, I couldn't move from the house without my wheelchair..."*

Helga Bicakcic's husband and her son are both physicians. Helga therefore, knew a great deal about her illness, and her kidneys, which were filling with kidney stones more than usual.
"For years I had difficulty sleeping. I felt as though somebody was pushing me and I would wake at 1:00 a.m. and fall asleep when the clock reached 4:00 a.m. As a result, during the day, I was tired, feeling as a million broken pieces." Since I started drinking Taheebo tea, in the past five nights, I never awakened. My family suggests that this was triggered by 'mind over matter' or 'autosuggestion.' Even if that be true, I am happy. It is such a good feeling to be able to sleep through the entire night... Also I noticed that my urinating has improved which is so good for my right kidney..."

Three days after she started to take Taheebo tea, Nevena Gaslic (26) contacted people at the address Djure Djakovica (41), where she bought it. She asked why she was sweating and shaking so much. Why she was hearing so many noises in her head. She could feel it on the spot, where earlier in her life, she had suffered a fractured skull.

This reaction is nothing unexpected when Taheebo is in question. In a way, these reactions are good, because Taheebo shows its proper function. The system is cleansing itself from poisons that have accumulated in our bodies. If some people do not experience such a reaction, it does not necessarily mean that it is not working in another hidden way.

DISAPPEARED PAIN

Victoria N. (72) from Zagreb, had her left breast removed 20 years ago. It was believed that the cancer had been removed with it. Last year, however, in a routine checkup, it was found that cancer attacked some vital organs of this retired physician. Strong painkillers soon lost the battle with her pain.

Victoria drank her first cup of Taheebo tea two weeks ago, to be more precise, after her girlfriend read in "Svijet" (World) about "herb for all occasions." Three days after that Victoria called her friend and said: *"From now on, first God, then Taheebo and you who urged me to take it...."*

Namely, the pain that this wellknown lady from Zagreb, a one time beauty queen, had endured with such difficulties, completely disappeared after a few litres of Taheebo tea that she had consumed. She threw away her cane.

Did a change occur in her organism, or in the organs affected by cancer? It is too early to say. The physician feels other improvement as well, but before she goes for her checkup, she doesn't wish to talk about it. Nevertheless, because of having been liberated from pain, she tells others: *"First God and then Taheebo..."*

Even 45 year old Nada Z. from Banja Luka wanted to stay incognito. More importantly is that she told us about her positive experience with Taheebo after which nobody can feel indifferent.

Five years ago she had a tumour removed from her head. Within two years her left breast was affected. Two years after that Nada found a new lump.

Because of her fears, she didn't follow through on checkups for more than four months. Just then, her husband brought her an unusual gift from abroad, a packet containing ten bags of tea. He received it from his business partner, who was a dedicated follower of healthy food and healthy lifestyle.

The basic instructions, how to prepare Taheebo were brief. Nada recalls that the sheet explained white men discovered this tea in 1977 only. Prior to that it was exclusively used by Callawaya tribes, descendants of the ancient Inca civilization. It was used for the cure of cancer, infections, rheumatism, gastritis, ulcers... The bark of this tree builds blood, awakens the body, enhancing development of new vital elements and new normal cells in the body, according to the instruction sheet. Quechua substances are simply antibiotics. It kills all bad microbes and brings the whole body in total defense readiness, it was said...

Two weeks after intensive consumption of Taheebo tea, many open sores appeared on Nada's body. They covered her entire body and were of different sizes. With that, a new fear entered her mind, but the first ray of hope as well.

Because the instruction sheet had said that the system is being liberated from many poisons, this calmed her somewhat. Within ten days the open sores disappeared and the lump disappeared also.

Only then, Nada went to see her physician. After a complete examination, he tapped her on the shoulder and told her that something mysterious and beautiful was happening in her system. Something that increased the number of her red blood cells, and normalized all her body construction.

FANTASTIC BLOOD PICTURE

Amila H. from Zenica, twenty-two years old, was told that she had cancer last year:

"I came to the hospital for a couple of days for some regular tests... On the eleventh day the head physician informed me, as we were casually walking along the corridor, as though a tooth extraction was in question. Tomorrow he had some free time and that it would be beneficial for me to make use of it, saying that he was not sure when I would have another opportunity to be fitted in for the surgery..."

"I was listening and heard and understood every word that he said. I looked at him speechlessly while he urged me, to "finally" decide if I will or will not allow amputation of my breast..."

Instead, Amila requested discharge papers from the hospital and went to Zagreb first, then to Ljubljana. The diagnosis was confirmed there, as well. According to them, there was no question that she had the worst type of cancer.

This brave young woman spent two months in Ljubljana. Chemotherapy was started, and implantation, a kind of radiation administered by needles pushed directly into the tumour.

Then Amila for the first time heard about Taheebo and started taking it and is still taking it to this day. Her checkups showed satisfactory results until February this year (1991). The doctors were totally surprised with what the biopsy showed. Another implant was suggested, others supported a more "classic" method. Some of the doctors, said that perhaps a mistake in the diagnosis was made from the beginning and that carcinoma wasn't present. Amili's excellent blood picture, contributed to these findings, as well as a psychophysical condition, characteristic of healthy people only. All over her perfectly tanned face were pimples. Pimples started breaking out, over the entire face and neck.

"I was sure that through them, everything bad was cleansing from my system..."

She drinks one litre of Taheebo tea every day. Regardless of what the next checkup will show, she decided to go on a macrobiotic diet, and what was more important, on a macrobiotic way of life. Taheebo fitted into this way of life.

Texts from "Svijet" (World) newspaper, prompted 54 years' old Danica A., from Ilidja to come to "EKOS" to by the tea:

"Three days after taking the tea, I could move my arm normally. Prior to that, I couldn't move it for a centimetre without enormous pain."

"At the same time a rush occurred, and for one entire evening I had a fit of shivering. I felt, that my toes were no longer cold as previously. I felt pain emanating from all the areas, where the reactions had occurred. From them I could predict the weather, better than any meteorologist could. Where I had broken my knee-

cap, as a child, I felt as though somebody was scraping over it...
This lasted three to four days and disappeared. Yes, the most
important thing is that I don't feel any more of my spondylitis, as
though it had never bothered me..."

SICKNESS STOPPED

Mato B. (84) from Sarajevo started to drink Taheebo tea. Within one week, his urine, which had always been bloody and murky, returned to a normal colour. The wrinkled face of this kidney patient also retained a normal colour:

"After such a long time I have again had a normal stool, I sleep peacefully and have a better appetite," stated this elderly man. The most important affirmation to his present healthy state he emphasizes, is that he is going out of the house alone, on his way to buy another bag of Taheebo.

Ljiljana Cukovic (49) from Sarajevo agreed to let us use her full name.

Last year cancer in her breast was discovered, and shortly after that, surgery was performed.

This cheerful witty lady, spoke calmly about her life story, as though she was speaking about someone else. We told her that we noticed this about her and she responded with a smile: *"My daughter told me recently: I can't believe that you are the same person..."*

She then went on to explain her state of peace within, which never changed, even last February. In that spot again, another lump was detected. It would only be natural for one to get upset and concerned. Following her surgery, she completely changed her diet. Ljiljana eliminated meat, fatty food, white sugar, and turned to more integral grains, vitamins and minerals. She was taking aloe as well, then herb pills, which she got from Kavadarac. Last February she started to take Taheebo:

"The last medical checkup showed that my blood picture is excellent, and that the lump remains. It is not increasing nor decreasing... I don't know if it is because of Taheebo tea, but I do know that my mental or emotional state, since I have been using it, is better then before, when I considered myself healthy... I feel as though it gives me some additional energy..."

I CAN'T BE WITHOUT TEA

Eight months ago Smiljka Kostovic from Sarajevo, was found to have a malignant tumour in her breast:

"I was looking for the truth about myself, and that way faced with the real world of sick people to which I belonged, I would surely get a chance to be healthy again."

She says it with a calm tone, slowly, as though in her story somebody else is a protagonist:

"It wasn't quite that way - thoughts crowded into my head, one worse than the other. The fear was closing and opening my vision. I became indecisive, and separated from my loved ones and even from within myself."

After the surgery for the removal of the lump, she heard about Taheebo for the very first time. She started using it immediately.

"The surgeon was surprised to see how my wounds were healing so quickly... I wasn't surprised. Taheebo gave me some strength, which eliminated my feelings of apathy, and weakness. I sweated profusely, from every part of my body. On the second day after release from the hospital, I could work around the house. I no longer had the problems with my bowels and they became

more regular. Considering the larger previous problems with my urination, the bacteria now showed only traces... I sleep well... and I can't be without Taheebo. I was recently out of Sarajevo but returned earlier than I was supposed to... only because of Taheebo. It feeds me with something wonderful. I have the feeling that it connects all my fibres, fills the emptiness, and causes a balance between what I can do and what I want..."

Comment: Medical checkups showed that Smiljka Kostovic is healthy. She will continue her checkups at her own convenience.

CONVINCED PHYSICIAN

"My husband, a physician his whole life, had a health problem. At 33 he had a tumour on his pituitary gland. This lasted for eleven years, as no right diagnosis was ever made. After surgery, he lived a normal life. From a dental treatment he got the B virus of hepatitis. His professor told him" : "Colleague, let us not be fooled. This is chronic, aggressive hepatitis, which will turn to cirrhosis of the liver."

WITH TEA - CAPSULES AND DROPS

"I read of Taheebo in your newspaper and ordered it from the "EKOS" store in Sarajevo. My husband took tea for twenty days, and the first positive results showed. His blood picture improved considerably, and within one month returned to normal. The Professor insisted on a liver biopsy. The result was negative. Cirrhosis disappeared."

"Please, if you write more about Taheebo, include the liver cure in its merit. I am sure it helps with cirrhosis too."

This letter was sent by Milka Zivojinovic, from Pozarevac. The experience of her neighbour, in the same letter said. She had breast surgery for carcinoma. After radiation, she had terrible pain in her arm. The pain disappeared after seven days, since she started to drink Taheebo tea.

Many phone calls and letters testified to the benefits given by Taheebo tea. People contacted "EKOS" store at Djure Djakovica 41. Mubera and Muhidin Ramic kept records in a record book.

They showed us Taheebo products: teas, capsules and concentrated drops. We asked what was the difference among these products.

The difference is only that the tea has to be brewed. Drops and capsules are ready. Capsules filled with pulverized Taheebo, are taken 3 to 4 a day. Concentrated drops can be taken 2 to 3 times daily as a syrup. One teaspoon is good for a half litre of the tea. Capsules and drops we recommend to patients with heart problems, and those who can't take large quantities of liquid.

For the more seriously sick people, as those with tumours, we recommend a combination of drops, capsules and tea.

We tried the drops, and they tasted as syrup, nothing unusual.

AUTHOR'S COMMENTS

There are many confusions how to prepare and take Taheebo. Preparation of the tea has to be the exact way I described earlier in this book. How strong one will make it depends on their case. The stronger the tea, the better. If unable to drink it strong, the honey or maple syrup has to be used for a sweetener. No sugar should be used. Drops are good if made with pure fruit alcohol. If

159   *Josip Gabre*

made by any other kind of alcohol I would not recommend it. Drops have to be taken under the tongue, as homeopaths and naturopaths' medicine are taken, and kept there several minutes. The longer the better. The Taheebo capsule is best taken if the capsule is open and its content poured under the tongue. When mixed with saliva the healing power is absorbed by the glands under the tongue and swallowed slowly as a mixture. Taheebo enemas are also recommended. It stimulates the colon, cleanses it and is absorbed by the glands to the liver.

When taken orally, with every sip, the mouth has to be swashed, especially the glands under the tongue. They are agitated and absorbed immediately and when mixed with saliva and swallowed, the glands in the stomach absorb it better.

DEPRESSION DISAPPEARED

We spoke with patients about their experience with Taheebo. A lady from Arilje, struggled unsuccessfully against uterus mynoma. Bleeding occurred every three to four days. The problem aggravated with leg swelling due to bad circulation. Capillaries were bursting, and toes became blue. Her kidneys did not function properly either. Then Taheebo came to the rescue. After only one month, fantastic changes happened. Bleeding diminished and then slowly disappeared. Enthusiastically, she says, the life is returning in her toes.

Among customers are many diabetics who drink Taheebo regularly. Many of them terminated to take insulin. A young lady suffered of depression for a long time. Her insomnia and unrest, she could only control with a handful of pills. She was desperate because the pills caused side effects. Her digestion was imperiled. Then she found Taheebo and started to drink the tea. *I feel as reborn again and am not using tablets anymore,"* she said.

IMPORTANCE OF NUTRITION

A young lady from Zrenjanin has breast cancer. She has been drinking Taheebo for three months now. After some time, her condition improved and her wounds started to clear. High pressure normalized and now she is very close to total recovery.

Improvement happened to a lady who had a pancreas tumour. Pain disappeared after several days, and high sedimentation lowered. A surprise to her physician, her blood picture got better, and so too is her health improving daily.

The Ramic family stresses proper nutrition. The best results were with patients who changed their diet. Meat is to be avoided, and the use of more integral grains, fruit and vegetables increased. Along with good healthy food, traditional medicine is recommended. The most important key is changing your way of life.

Dr. Goran Sulejmanovic, a radiologist from the Institute of Radiology and Oncology in Sarajevo, investigates alternate medicine. We showed him the case of Marko S. In the hospital in Ljubljana, Marko was diagnosed with lung carcinoma. Surgery was impossible due to his sickness progression. Then Marko heard about Taheebo, and received his first quantity from Peru. Very soon he became more vital and walked out of the house. His blood picture improved considerably. A general checkup, several days ago, confirmed cancer's withdrawal.

"We should never turn a blind eye to the possibility that something out of the orthodox can help. Regardless of what we think, traditional folk medicine always makes its way" says Dr. Sulejmanovic.

For lupus crytematodase, the system disease, the cause is unknown. One lady, stricken by that disease, was taking Taheebo tea for twenty days. Her general condition considerably improved.

161   *Josip Gabre*

That lady from Sarajevo, within two and a half years, suffered lots of pain. First in the hospital, she was said to have rheumatoid arthritis. When her doctors realised that her diagnosis was wrong, they concluded that her liver was damaged. That too was wrong. Only one year ago, lupus was indentified. Complete exhaustion and tiredness are symptoms of that disease. Drinking Taheebo, the patient felt as if her joints were warming up. Itching occurred on the skin, above the joints, then numbness slowly disappeared. Again, she could do her housework.

Concerning this case, Dr. Sulemanpasic is pointing to the complementary use of Taheebo with medicine in many cases of illness. Taheebo does not exclude radiation or even cyto-therapy. In such cases when antibiotics are taken with Taheebo tea, results are even better. Obviously, here, this happened with lupus.

All of this speaks for itself. The "Holy Tree" as it was called by the Inca tribes, was in many labs confirmed to have therapeutic value. In our part of the world, Taheebo brought cures to people when hope vanished. This is the reason, that we now write about Taheebo for the third time.

The truth cannot and will not be denied.

LETTER TO "EKOS"
(the Health-food store)

Dear Madam

On this occasion, please, accept my deepest esteem. I wish, your continued success in helping those in need.

As an expression of my thanks, I wish to describe, one of many successful healings with Taheebo.

My Father-in-law got ill in the beginning of 1991. He had leukemia of the third degree, with 82,000 white blood corpuscles. In medical terms this is so high a rating, patients are written off. The normal number of white blood corpuscles are between 6,000 and 8,000. Every day his condition was worsening. In the newspaper "The Third Eye" I found an article on Taheebo or the "Holy Tree." I ordered it from you, had my Father-in-law use it according to the instructions and his success after ten days, was unbelievable.

His number of white blood corpuscles rapidly went down to 8,200, the equivalent of a healthy baby. My Father-in-law is 67 years old.

Besides leukemia he was very nervous. He could not sleep, and had lost his desire to live.

Along with Taheebo tea, he used horse meat (100 grams daily), drank red beet juice, ate raw carrots and plenty of fruits. Although he used all of that before, improvement happened only when he started to drink Taheebo.

Therefore, please, tell everybody, Taheebo is a beneficial herb for many illnesses. I am telling that to everybody too. To these unhappy people you do a big favour. By helping them, many, you made happy. If anybody is happy about it, surely you are, meaning, Mubera and Muhidin together.

Thank you very much.

Sincerely yours:

Rajko Janjic

Josip Gabre

Mrs. Sylvia Seidel
R.R.#1
Cameron, Ont.
KOM 1GO
May 11, 1994

Dear Mr. Gabre,

I have just received the package containing taheebo bark
and instructions which you have so kindly sent me. I am
overwhelmed by the selflessness and generosity you show in
helping complete strangers, and I hope you will accept the
enclosed cheque to help cover your expenses. Please let me
know if it is not enough.

As a registered nurse I work in and am comfortable with
the world of modern medicine, however I believe my mind is open
enough to explore and accept the great value of the traditional
medicine of other cultures. It is frightening that scientists
seem to turn blind eyes to the many benefits which exist in
nature.

I have many unanswered questions and I hope you can help
me with a few of them when you have time. First, I am going
to complete my chemotherapy for breast cancer this June – should
I wait til then before starting to take taheebo? Also, where
can I get more taheebo? I have relatives in Mississauga who
can help, and a friend who owns a health food store who could
order it for me if she knew where it is available. And I am
very interested in additional information such as articles,
research studies, etc. I'm a little confused about the tea
instructions. Is it one tablespoon of bark per litre of water?

Once again, thankyou so much for your help. I look forward
to hearing from you again and I have also enclosed a self
addressed and stamped envelope to help.

Sincerely yours,

Sylvia Seidel

(705-887-6414)

April 27, 1994.

Gary Jenkins,
147 Springdale Drive,
Barrie, Ontario,
L4M 4Y1.

Mr. Josip Gabre,
4523 The Gallops,
Mississauga, Ontario,
L5M 3B3.

Dear Josip;
    I have read most of your book already, and I feel that I know
you personally! Thanks for your prompt mailing of this most
important message. As you are aware, this is a story that seems to
have, or will, effect most of us. Just about the time you were
starting your ordeal, my dad was in T.G.H. on his last stand after
a two year fight with the hyperthermia treatment. His Dr. was Rudy
Faulk.   As you know, this type of battle is seldom won.

If only we had known at that time, what you know now.
            THIS IS VERY IMPORTANT INFORMATION TO BE PASSED ON.
As I get older, 56 now, I'll have to re:read the book a few times
to get the full effect and understanding.   But, I have a few
questions already.

1. Where does one get Taheebo Tea ?   Approx. cost ?

2. Since I have lost my Dad, an Aunt, and another Uncle opperated
on with cancer, It's in the family. Would one cup a day be a
preventative idea for myself ?

3. How do you market this valuable book ?   Book stores ?

Enclosed is a cheque for $34.20.   Please send me two more copies.

You'll find my name on the enclosed cards, and look at our
company's name. Is there another touch of destiny here ? Yes
Josip, I will meet you soon.
God be with you,

Regards,

Gary Jenkins

165   *Josip Gabre*

July 5, 1994.

Dear Mr. Gabre,

I heard about your Tahebo tea from my uncle, Wilfrid Doyon, he was near death until he started drinking your Tahebo tea, we couldn't believe the change in him. I would like some of your Tahebo tea, and would gladly pay for it. I'm sure it would help my husband's back and arms.

I'm so looking forward in hearing from you.

Sincerely

Joan Cayen

R.R. 1
Warren Ont.
P0H-2N0

P.S. I also read some of your book and found it very interesting.

Aug. 5/ 1994

346 ANNE ST. N.
BARRIE, ONTARIO
L4N 5M9

I HAVE TO APOLOGIZE FOR TAKING SO LONG IN MAILING
YOU YOUR MONEY ORDER. I HAVE YOUR REMARKABLE BOOK
NOT TOO FAR FROM MY HAND & THERE IS NEVER A DAY THAT
THAT I DO NOT MENTION YOUR BOOK TO SOMEONE ON HOW YOU
BEAT CANCER. I PICK IT UP AND READ SOME EVERY DAY, OR
THINK ABOUT YOU & YOUR FAMILY GOD BLESS YOU ALL !.
I WILL KEEP IN TOUCH.
THANK YOU FOR SENDING ME YOUR BOOK. MONEY ORDER ENCLOSED.

YOURS SINCERELY

E. L. MacInnes
EILEEN LEE MACINNES

Josip Gabre

Dear Josip

Thank you for sending the Jaheeko Tea which I am faithfully taking every day & finding myself feeling better each day. I know this tea is helping in riding my body of those cancer cells.

Enclosed is a cheque for the Tea & I will continue to be in touch with you.

Lenore Millar.

RR 3, Bracebridge,
Ontario, P1L 1X1.

May 12, 1994

Telephone: 705-645-4091

Mr Josip Gabre,
4523 The Gallops,
MISSISSAUGA, Ontario,
L5M 3B3.

Dear Mr. Gabre:

I wish to thank you very much for forwarding to me your book
entitled "How I Beat Cancer". It is a very interesting book
which I have read from cover to cover. Actually when I phoned
you requesting information all I expected was a pamphlet so
I was very surprised that you would send me your book.

Like you we have seen the adverse effect of the administering
of chemotherapy to some of the people we know. It is too
bad that the Taheebo tea is not given more consideration by
the medical profession. Likewise Rene Caise was up against
a "blank wall" with the medical profession with her Essiac.
We have personaly seen the adverse effect of modern drugs due
to their side affects and yet they don't seem to want to
bother to give either the taheebo tea or Essiac a fair trial.
Granted it may not help everyone but at least give it a try.

I am enclosing a bank money order for $12.00 to cover the
cost of your book, again I wish to express my apprecation
for your kindness. I hope it will cover your cost.

Your truly,

Evelyn Lambert

(Mrs.) Evelyn Lambert.

Wendy Thompson
Box 162
Orillia, ON
L3V 6J3
(705)689 8956

Josip Gabre
4523 The Gallops
Mississauga, ON
L5M 3B3

Dear Mr. Gabre,

I would like to graciously thank you for quickly sending the two pounds of tea and your book. I have much faith that this will greatly assist my Mother-In-Law in regaining her health. She has suffered with Chrones Disease for several years, has had several operations in which parts of her large and small intestines were removed. This method of treatment has yet to give her relief in fact it appears to slowly be taking away years as well as quality from her life.

The day I received your package, I rushed home with incredible excitement ~~excitement~~ and eagerly began reading it, this is hard to do though, as I have a very active five year old daughter named Stephanie.

Your personal journey in seeking and finding a cure is extremely motivating.

Through my reading your book many emotions were felt. Its interesting how we can shed tears for many emotions both sad and happy.

I have enjoyed your book for its content as well as for your wonderful writing abilities and would like to know more about your other writing projects,ie.-The Bread, Before The Storm and The Seed From The Stone

I would also like to know how best to store the tea. Would a glass jar be suitable or should I leave it in the bags in which you sent it? As well I would like to ask you when more tea is needed would I be able to call on you to send it?

Again, dear sir, I thank you for sharing your story as well as others and for your knowledge of this tea.

Sincerely,

Wendy Thompson

Wendy Thompson

How I beat cancer   **170**

REFERENCES

ANTHONY J. SATTILARO, TOM MONTE. Recalled By Life. Avon Books, New York 1982.

BAILEY, HERBERT. A matter of Life and Death: The Incredible Story of Krebiozen. New York: G.P. Putnam's Sons, 1958.

BARD, MORTON. "The Price of Survival for Cancer Victims." In Where Medicine Fails, edited by Anselm Strauss. New Brunswick, N.J.; Transaction Books, 1973.

BARRY, LYNES. *The Healing of Cancer.* The Cures - the Cover-ups and the Solution Now! Marcus Books, Queensville, Ontario, Canada 1989.

BARRY, LYNES. *The Cancer Cure That Worked!* Fifty years of suppression. Marcus Books, Queensville, Ontario, Canada 1987, 1989.

BOESCH, MARK. *The Long Search for the Truth About Cancer.* New York: G. P. Putnam's Sons, 1960.

BRODEUR, PAUL. *Expendable Americans.* New York: Viking Press, 1974. [Excellent study of the asbestos problem by a *New Yorker* reporter.]

BRODY, JANE AND HOLLEB ARTHUR. *You Can Fight Cancer and Win.* New York: Times Books, 1977.

CAMERON, EWAN AND PAULING, LINUS. *Cancer and Vitamin C*. Menlo Park: Linus Pauling Institute of Science and Medicine, 1979. [Bookstore distribution by W. W. Norton & Co., New York. The basic text on theory of ascorbic acid's effect on cancer.]

CHOWKA, PETER BARRY. "An Interview with Dr. Gio Gori." *East West,* January 1978.

CHOWKA, PETER BARRY. "The National Cancer Institute and the Fifty-Year Cover-Up." *East West,* January 1978b. [One in a series of provocative essays by a bright young critic of establishment medicine.]

CHOWKA, PETER BARRY. "The Cancer Charity Rip-Off." *East West,* July 1978c.

CRILE, GEORGE, JR. *What Women Should Know About the Breast Cancer Controversy*. New York: Pocket Books, 1974. [Simply written but powerful argument against radical mastectomy, by a leading surgeon.]

CULBERT, MICHAEL. *Freedom from Cancer*. Seal Beach. Calif.: '76 Press, 1976.

D'ANGIO, GIULIO J. "Pediatric Cancer in Perspective: Cure Is Not Enough." *Cancer* 35(3), March 1975.

EPSTEIN, SAMUEL S. *The Politics of Cancer*. San Francisco: Sierra Club Books, 1978 (rev. ed. Garden City, N.Y.: Anchor Press/Doubleday, 1979). [Exhaustive study of environmental carcinogens by a leading advocate of prevention].

FINK, JOHN M. *Third Opinion: An International directory of alternative Therapy Centers for the Treatment and prevention of Cancer*. Garden City Park, N. Y.: Avery Publishing Group, Inc., 1988.

FRAUMENI, JOSEPH F., Jr. ed. *Persons at High Risk of Cancer.* New York: Academic Press, 1975.

GERSHANOVICH, M. L.; FILOV, V.A. "Hydrazine Sulfate in Late Stage Cancer: Completion of Initial Clinical Trials in 225 Evaluable Patients."

GERSHANOVICH, M. L.; DANOVA, L. A.; IVIN, B. A.; and FILOV. V. A. "Results of Clinical Study of Antitumor Action of Hydrazine Sulfate." *Nutrition and Cancer* 3:7-12, 1981

GLEMSER, BERNARD. *Man Against Cancer.* New York: Funk and Wagnalls, 1969.

GREEN, SAUL, "Cancer and Surveillance by the Immune System in Man," *Cope,* April/May, 1989.

GREENBERG, DANIEL S. "A Critical Look at Cancer Coverage." *Columbia Journalism Review,* January-February 1975.

GRIFFIN, G. EDWARD. *World Without Cancer:* The Story of Vitamin B-17. Thousand Oaks, Calif.: American Media, 1975.

HOFFMAN, FREDERICK L. *Cancer and Diet.* Baltimore: Williams and Wilkins Company, 1937.

HOWARD, N. WAGAR. *How I Cured Myself of Cancer.* A testimony. Alive Books.

ISRAEL, LUCIEN. *Conquering Cancer.* New York: Random House, 1978.

ISSELS, J. *Cancer: A Second Opinion*. London: Hodder and Stoughton, 1975.

JAN DE VRIES. *Cancer and Leukemia - an Alternative approach*. Billing & Sons Ltd. Worcester G. B.

KEDAR, N. PRASAD. *Vitamins Against Cancer*. Healing Art Press, Rochester, Vermont 1984, 1989.

LOUISE, GREENFIELD. *Cancer Overcome by Diet* An alternative to surgery. Midwest Publishing Co. Livonia Mich.

MARY RUTH SWOPE.
MICHIO, KUSHI, ALEX JACK. *The Cancer Prevention Diet*. St. Martin's Press, New York.

MICHIO, KUSHI. *The Macrobiotic Approach to Cancer*. Avery Publishing Group Inc. Wayne, New Jersey.
MORRIS, NAT. *The Cancer Blackout*. Los Angeles: Regent House, 1977. [A history of unorthodox approaches to cancer.]

MOSS, RALPH W. *The Cancer Syndrome*. New York: Grove Press, 1980.

MOSS, RALPH W. *The Cancer Industry*. Unravelling the Politics. Paragon House 1989.

MOSS, RALPH W. The Promise of Hydrazine Sulfate." *Penthouse,* January 1983.

NULL, GARY. "The suppression of Cancer Cures." *Penthouse*, October 1979.